Leading the Future:
The Human Science of Law Firm Strategy and Leadership

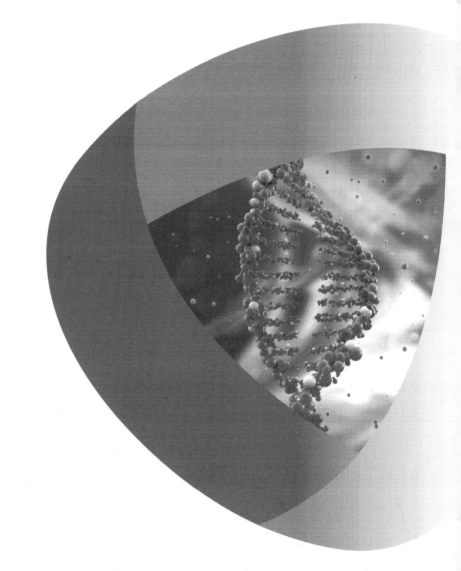

DR BOB MURRAY AND
DR ALICIA FORTINBERRY

Head of legal publishing
Fiona Fleming

Publisher
Helen Donegan

Managing editor
Emma Reitano

Editor
Laura Slater

Published by ARK Group:

UK, Europe and Asia office
6–14 Underwood Street
London, N1 7JQ
United Kingdom
Tel: +44(0) 207 566 5792
publishing@ark-group.com

North America office
4408 N. Rockwood Drive, Suite 150
Peoria IL 61614
United States
Tel: +1 (309) 495 2853
publishingna@ark-group.com

www.ark-group.com

Layout by Susie Bell, www.f-12.co.uk

Printed by Canon (UK) Ltd, Cockshot Hill, Reigate, RH2 8BF, United Kingdom

ISBN: 978-1-78358-231-0

A catalogue record for this book is available from the British Library

ARK Group is a division of Wilmington plc. The company is registered in England & Wales
with company number 2931372 GB
Registered office: 6-14 Underwood Street, London N1 7JQ. VAT Number: GB 899 3725 51.

Contents

Executive summary

We have all been told how artificial intelligence, computers, digitization, decomposition, and robotics are going to decimate law firms and make most lawyers unemployed. This may be true, but the future has a funny way of not turning out as predicted.

We have become entranced with what machines can do. They can solve legal problems, make predictions and better diagnoses than the best and most experienced doctors, and – according to one report – will eventually render 90 percent of accountants redundant. This is all due to the exponential growth in computing technology and mathematics.

In this book, we look at the business of law from the perspective of a different set of sciences: the human sciences of psychology; behavioral neurogenetics; biological psychiatry; anthropology; and neuroscience. Groundbreaking new research in these areas has dramatic implications for all areas of life and represents humanity's most exciting new frontier. In terms of leading law firms, it is showing us that there are different, vastly more efficient, and yet more human-centric ways of working together, and of leading, marketing, and selling.

Science tells us that the product that lawyers are selling is not, and never has been, law. It shows that it does not matter if the practice of law itself is obliterated, because what will take its place is a profession that lawyers are uniquely suited to occupy.

Each of the chapters in this book develops from a basic premise that has been proven by a vast body of research over the last 10 years or so: humans are relationship-forming animals and in everything that we do, in all the work we perform and all the things we make, sell, and distribute, we have one essential objective, which is to surround ourselves with a nexus of supportive relationships. The most recent research has added considerably to our understanding of what this really means.

It is not that we can outdo machines at performing tasks; we cannot. We cannot make better predictions or analyze big data faster or more efficiently. However, we can use what we the authors call "human science" – the wisdom of all those sciences – to construct firms that sell services with a legal focus. Because those services are based on how humans really work and what humans really want, clients will really need and will be willing to pay for them.

We can also manage our firms much more efficiently by working with our people in ways that will enable them to do their jobs better, more collaboratively, and with greater flexibly. The new way of working will allow for increased innovation and staff engagement. There will be improved trust between people at all levels. The enthusiasm with which people work together will, as the research shows, draw clients to the firm. In terms of marketing – when applied to clients, prospective clients, and stakeholders – "human science" enables law leaders to ask the questions that will lead the way to far greater results, and even a new way of looking at the business they are in.

The 15 chapters in this book examine how human science interacts with different aspects of leading, managing, and marketing in a law firm. The book is very practical in focus, with tools and tips that you can immediately put into practice. We, the authors, have deep experience in applying the latest science to business challenges. We are therefore uniquely qualified to guide you to shape a successful strategy and drive positive change through the right leadership, culture, business development, and customer relationships for your legal business. Our experience is shared liberally throughout this book in the form of actionable guidance, backed up by hard facts.

Chapter 1 looks at the future for law firms from the perspective of, on the one hand, a futurist who envisages a world where law will be largely the province of artificial intelligence, the internet, and robotics; and, on the other hand, from the point of view of human science. It's not that the two conflict; it's just that they point to differing outcomes. One is fairly pessimistic with lawyers reduced essentially to IT professionals; in the other, there is a whole new service that lawyers are, perhaps uniquely, able to provide. How do we lead the law firm of the future in such a way as to make the best of the new opportunities that will arise? Again, human science points the way to something different. It points to needing new skills and offering people in the firm a new and more autonomous way of working.

Chapter 2 examines strategy. Not any particular strategy, but the best way of making strategy work. Our premise is that, currently, between 70–90 percent of all strategic initiatives fail to achieve their goals. In this chapter, we look closely at the reasons behind this failure rate. We examine what human science has to say about the best way of going about formulating strategy. We look at questions such as: What really is strategic thought? What role should game theory play? Who are the best people to devise a new strategy? What is the role of big data in formulating strategy? What are the pitfalls that stop leaders from doing the right things in formulating strategy?

Chapter 3 covers leadership. How should firms be led in the era of the "new normal", of constant change and innovation? Most law firms are managed in ways that prevent them from taking advantage of the opportunities that are arising. Human science shows managing partners and other law leaders how to get the most from their people, how to get them committed to the leader, to the firm, and to the strategy of the firm. It shows the simple techniques that law leaders can use to ensure a high level of engagement, flexibility, and innovation.

Chapter 4 deals with decision making. In particular, we show that the usual ways we go about making decisions – weighing all the evidence, relying on our past experience, looking at the relevant facts and figures – are all somewhat suboptimal. This chapter looks at how decisions are actually made in the brain, and what are the influencers of those decisions. We examine the role of emotions and our "perceptual filter", the network of beliefs and assumptions (most of which are misguided) that tend to lead us to make bad choices. We look at what really works, how the best decisions are made, and how you can use this knowledge to vastly improve the accuracy of your decision making.

Chapter 5 is about getting the right culture in place to drive innovation and change. It offers practical tips and suggestions about how to lead culture change and how to get your people engaged in the process. In this chapter we outline how you can get your people engaged in creating the right culture, and how you can build that culture around a vision and mission that they can subscribe to. We emphasize the importance of concentrating on specific behaviors, rather than trying to build a culture around vague statements of values. We show that there is a right time to lead in culture creation and a right time to step back and let the new culture evolve. We guide you through the process.

Chapter 6 is about getting commitment to change. Most organizations, and people, resist change. It goes through the same brain pathways as physical pain – it hurts! In this chapter we look at ways to carry out successful change. We look at the false assumptions that most leaders have which can derail innovation and change. We look at the use, and misuse, of influencers. We give practical tips which will make it easy to overcome "change fright" in individuals and firms, and share ways to make change stick.

Chapter 7 outlines how to create and inspire high-performing teams. Teams are much more effective than individuals in almost all areas of human endeavor. But there is something really rare and special about genuinely high-performing teams (HPTs). It is these that every firm wants and needs in order to successfully navigate the future. In this chapter we look at the science of high performance and the practical lessons that can be taken from this new knowledge in order to create and inspire HPTs. We also take a closer look at the key things that determine high performance in teams: HPT dialogue, and the concept of leaderless teams. It is these that distinguish HPTs from the rest.

Chapter 8 examines the how-to of effective persuasion. Over the last couple of years neuroscience and behavioral neurogenetics have taught us a huge amount about how to persuade and influence people. Effective persuasion is, of course, vital in selling our services, leading our people, and changing and growing our firms. We examine what the latest research says about influence and persuasion – what does and what does not persuade. You will find that many of the techniques you currently use to try to persuade people are actually counter-productive and switch people off, no matter what they say. We look at the real hidden persuaders – not the ones which, up until a few years ago, people cited. We show how it is possible to discover what people's real needs are so that you can target them more accurately – without the need for big data. We end the chapter with the "10 commandments" of effective persuasion. Many of them will surprise you.

Chapter 9 is about driving trust at all levels. Most law firms are deficient in trust. These days the authors are asked more often to help in building trust and cooperation than anything else. Recently, researchers have discovered the real drivers of trust in human beings, what gets the trust neurochemical, oxytocin, really flowing to the right parts of the system. In this chapter, we go through the how-to of creating and sustaining trust throughout the firm. We show you how to powerfully use what we call the "five Cs" of trust, which science and our own experience prove can increase the level of trust in any relationship, or any organization.

Chapter 10 is about the how-to of powerful dialogue. Research shows that there are six essential characteristics of dialogue. We use words not just to convey information, but more importantly to tell people about ourselves. We use conversation to discover commonalities which encourage trust, we use it to find out other people's needs and to convey our own, and we use it to make people feel loyal and committed to us. Yet the truth is that we don't hear over 60 percent of what other people are saying. We are too busy formulating our own answers, putting forward our own points of view, thinking our own thoughts, getting caught up in our own fears. This chapter shows not only how to use good dialogue skills, but how to genuinely hear what other people are saying. We also give you the how-to of asking the powerful questions which will get to the heart of the matter, whatever you're talking about.

Chapter 11 is about effective collaboration and cooperation. In our experience, most law firms are not good at collaboration. In fact, they vary from being fairly good at it, to being appalling. This applies whether the collaborators are in one place, or spread virtually throughout the world, or even where the firm has no fixed offices at all. In this chapter, we show that in all of these situations you can build an engaged and compelling tribe. We show how you can encourage cross-selling, resolve conflicts, and even build collaborative relationships with your clients. You can encourage your partners and lawyers, wherever they are, to work as a committed team.

Chapter 12 shows how to reward people in meaningful ways without simply resorting to paying them more. In the future, law firms will have to find ways of rewarding people without continuously paying them more money. One of the things that science shows is that money is not a great motivator; there are much better ones. In this chapter we show the how-to of devising and using non-material rewards, and in particular how to use what we call "relational rewards". By using these skillfully, law leaders can drive performance, increase engagement, and increase the happiness that people derive from working in their firms.

Chapter 13 delves into how research dictates you should hire and promote the right people. Who are the right people for your firm? How do you select for the traits that will give you the right balance? Who should you promote? Should you select for diversity in all areas, or for commonality? Are there a few simple rules that you can follow which will get you through this minefield? Fortunately there are, and the more we know about how the human system works, the clearer they become. This chapter gives you the answers to the questions you need to ask before you set out to hire anybody, as well as how to pick out those who will meet your needs and will become truly engaged employees.

Chapter 14 outlines how to create an optimistic firm. Optimistic firms are more productive and profitable. We the authors are amongst the foremost experts on creating optimism at work and in families, having written two best-selling books and many, many articles on the subject. Our own and other people's research over the past several years has revealed a lot more about how law leaders can create an optimistic work environment and reduce the incidence of depression and other mood disorders. We will explore the five elements of creating optimism, and give you practical advice and guidance on how to implement them.

Chapter 15 asks a fundamental question: What are you really selling? It looks at the business of law firms and concludes that their business is not law, but something quite different. We delve into the very latest findings in human science to outline what people are really willing to buy, and why. We look at the drivers of all purchasing decisions. We find that what people are really buying when they enter the doors (real or virtual) of your firm does not include law. We conclude that, in fact, law firms have never been in the business of law. This realization leads to an even greater one: lawyers are uniquely qualified to sell a service that every businessperson and every corporate and government leader wants and needs. Instead of a pessimistic vision of the end of lawyers, we arrive at a totally different conclusion which can change the whole nature of what laws firms are about. This chapter is a how-to of the future.

About the authors

Bob Murray, MBA, PhD (Clinical Psychology), is an internationally recognized expert in strategy, leadership, human personality, and behavioral change. Distinguished for his ability to uncover the core of issues, Bob has developed ground-breaking methods for measuring, benchmarking, and improving an organization's capacity for change and adaptation.

Bob's insights are based on his wide experience and also on his deep knowledge of research in the areas of management, psychology, genetics, and neurobiology. Clients include premier law firms such as Allens Linklaters, Ashurst, and Herbert Smith Freehills; and other top tier companies such as KPMG, Macquarie Bank, PwC, Ford, Caterpillar, McDonald's, PepsiCo, BHP, Wesfarmers, and Stockland.

Bob is an acclaimed keynote speaker and is widely published. With Dr Alicia Fortinberry, Bob received the American Science Achievement Award (2012) and advises the US government on workplace stress and other workplace issues. He specializes in ensuring executive teams develop and drive strategies that will be embraced and actioned.

Bob's previous experience includes working for Hill Samuel Merchant Bank, where he helped to turn around distressed companies, as well as working as a BBC producer. With Alicia, he authored the best-selling books *Creating Optimism* and *Raising an Optimistic Child* (McGraw-Hill). These international best-sellers have become standards in the fields of optimism and resilience.

Bob has lectured at Sydney, Duke, Tufts, South Florida, and California State universities. He received his MBA from Sydney University (where he also earned his MA in Psychology) and his PhD from New York University.

Bob is a member of the American Psychological Association, the American Association for the Advancement of Science, and the American Society of Journalists and Authors.

Alicia Fortinberry, PhD (Organizational Psychology) has gained international recognition over two decades for her powerful, lasting impact on organizations and leaders globally. Alicia enables organizations to build the leadership, performance, and culture that will achieve their vision and strategy. In addition to her work as a consultant, facilitator, and high-level executive coach, Alicia is a best-selling author and keynote speaker. She combines a clear, engaging, and practical communication style with a proven evidence-based approach and strategic acumen.

With her highly experienced and credentialed Fortinberry Murray team, Alicia works with organizations and governments globally to help leaders shape and implement winning strategies using research-based understanding of human motivation and change.

With her colleague Dr Bob Murray, Alicia won the American Science Achievement Award (2012) and has been appointed to head the US government's comprehensive national work stress initiative.

Alicia's pioneering work is backed by the latest research in neuroscience, genetics, and management. Together with Bob, she has presented her work at leading universities such as Duke, Tufts, California State, and Sydney University.

High level global clients include professional and financial services firms such as Deloitte, KPMG, PwC, Macquarie, Westpac, Allens Linklaters, Clayton Utz, and Herbert Smith Freehills, as well as companies such as Stockland, Wesfarmers, Westpac, BHP, Macdonald's, PepsiCo, and Ford.

With Bob she authored the best-selling books *Creating Optimism* and *Raising an Optimistic Child* (McGraw-Hill). These international bestsellers have become standards in the fields of optimism and resilience.

Alicia received her Masters in Psychology and Journalism from Columbia University and her PhD in Organizational Psychology from the University of Phoenix. She is a member of the American Psychological Association, the American Association for the Advancement of Science, and the American Society of Journalists and Authors.

Acknowledgements

We (Bob and Alicia) would like first of all to thank our clients and friends in the legal profession around the world who have offered their invaluable insights during the writing of this book, and who have helped us to gain the knowledge and understanding that underpin it over the many years we have worked with them.

Thanks also to Helen Donegan, publisher at the UK-based ARK Group, for your guidance and patience during the birthing process.

Laura Slater, editor at ARK, didn't just do a great job of copyediting; her positive comments were a great encouragement and source of dopamine.

Vivienne Coumbis, who runs the Fortinberry Murray offices and our lives, helped keep us on track with the various revisions, correspondence, and images. She is also a constant source of dopamine and oxytocin.

Chapter 1:
The future of the business of law

This chapter considers:

- What law firms will look like 10–15 years from now;
- The services lawyers of the future will provide; and
- The role firm leaders will play.

For the last few thousand years, the business of law has remained pretty much the same. Law has been a kind of guild in which the practitioners have reserved unto themselves a body of knowledge, and on the basis of that knowledge they have dispensed advice, rather like a medical doctor diagnoses a problem on the basis of their knowledge and gives the patient a prescription. Both the lawyer and the doctor have traditionally been "keepers of knowledge".

For both physicians and lawyers, those days are passing and will soon be gone for good. Knowledge, via the internet search engine, is now the common currency of the masses. Like the weavers after the invention of the spinning jenny, the holders of knowledge must find a new relevancy. One of the attributes of a great managing partner or CEO of a law firm is the ability to look into the future and visualize what their firm will be like 10–15 years from now.

In his book *Death of the Lawyer*, law futurist Richard Susskind says that besides globalization there are currently three drivers of change in law firms: cost pressure, liberalization, and technology. We would argue that this is certainly correct, but that there is another driver of change – the new knowledge coming out of the various sciences of human behavior.

In the course of this book, we want to look at both the future and the present in the light of these sciences. The ones which will inform much of what we say are behavioral neurogenetics, neurobiology, neurochemistry, psychology, and anthropology. Collectively, they tell us how to understand the real needs of clients, predict future trends, allow for the best combination of people and technology, and manage people to get them to perform at their best. This is the how-to of the future.

What will law firms look like?

To begin with, let's look at what a major law firm might look like 10–15 years from now. Of course, what we can perhaps all agree on is that it won't be the same as it is today! Whatever we put here won't be accurate.

Predicting the future is a necessary, but chancy, function for any organization. For example, if you are a planner in the US State Department, you play with a number of possible scenarios. These might include larger global issues such as economic, climate, and social change, as well as the more specific ones such as the European Union disintegrating, China or Russia splitting into a number of separate states, or civil war breaking out in South Africa. Each of these is looked at in depth and the options for the US are explored. Any law firm leadership should do a similar exercise at regular intervals because doing so will help them to devise a number of strategies to cope with any of the contingencies they envisage, should they arise. It will also get them used to concentrating on and planning for the future rather than viewing the present and the future through the lens of the past.

Many firms already do this, Herbert Smith Freehills being a prime example. Surprisingly, some don't. Many see strategic thinking as a one-off exercise instead of a continuous process. Some also see the present as part of a cycle which will, somehow, revert to the more comfortable times of the past. It won't. The new normal is constant flux.

So, let's take a look at a possible future of the major law firm 10–15 years down the track. Bear in mind that we are just projecting current trends into the future and the butterfly may yet flap its wings in Tibet and everything may change. Many of the routine offerings that firms used to provide have disappeared – they have been outsourced, in-housed, or broken down and made into software. In the future, we believe law will no longer be the prime offering of most of what are now "law firms". Under pressure from the Big 4 accounting firms – PwC, KPMG, Deloitte, and EY, who will all have developed legal practices as part of their one-stop-shop offering – law, and even legal advice of a high order, will have become thoroughly commoditized. It will no longer be profitable for this to be the sole offering of a "law" firm.

Current trends seem to indicate that just like the large plaintiff-law corporation Slater and Gordon, most if not all major firms will have become corporations, the majority of them listed on the London, New York, Shanghai, or Sydney exchanges. This will allow them to raise the funds and be flexible enough to better compete with the Big 4. The idea of partnership might hang on in some form in some of these ex-firms, but the reality is that the "partners" will have long since become employees rather than owners of the business.

By this time, almost all service-related businesses will have become virtual. This will also be true of legal businesses. The magnificent offices will have vanished; for most there will be no physical presence. The software to establish and run a virtual law firm already exists and some US high-end virtual firms, such as Rimon PC, have already become pretty large.

This trend will spread up the food chain to the Wall Street giants and the Magic Circle as the search for cost-saving becomes more and more imperative. In many of these businesses the lawyers will simply be self-employed individuals working principally, but not always exclusively, for one business.

The argument against this is that, for certain high-brand firms, there will always be a market for a law practice that helps clients solve the most intricate of problems and whose advice, in these circumstances, is "beyond value". That may be true, and there may be room for 10 or more such firms in the world, but looking ahead 10 years or so, on all serious current projections, that's it.

Open plan offices and agile workplaces will be seen for what they are: steps towards the elimination of offices altogether. The 10 firms mentioned above may still, quaintly, have offices – for all others, the cloud will be the office, the means of communication, the storage place for data, the place for knowledge management, and the place where the team, the "tribe" of lawyers that makes up the company, meets.

In-house corporate lawyers will be a thing of the past. Almost everything that they currently do will be decomposed, disaggregated, broken down into its component parts, and either farmed out, digitized, or swept up into AI. The dialogue will no longer be lawyer-to-lawyer, but rather lawyer-to-business function head, or even lawyer-to-CEO or COO.

And of course, above all else, client demands will have changed. Clients too will be swimming in a sea of rapid technological innovation, little growth, increasing regulation, declining employment driving cost and pricing pressures, digitization, low profits, and a rapidly changing economic environment. They will need guides who can help them navigate these waters. Unless the present law firms are very clever, it will be the Big 4 who provide the guidance.

Fortunately, the human behavioral sciences have vital things to say about coping with all of this and helping firms to meet future challenges, whatever they turn out to be. As the legendary ice hockey player Wayne Gretsky famously advised: "skate to where the puck is going to be, not where it has been".

What will lawyers do?

If the future is not likely to require the law in the traditional sense of the word, what will all the lawyers of the future be doing? The employees of legal businesses can only provide services that people are willing to buy. Therefore, we would ask a more fundamental question: What will people be buying? In reality, the business of law is a function of something else. People don't buy law – there is no market for law as such, and there never was. Only lawyers, or law students, are interested enough in the law to buy it.

Over the last few years, scientists and psychologists have discovered more about how the human system works and the prime human motivators than we learned in the previous 1.5 million years of our existence. One of the things we have discovered is that there are only four things that humans want enough to buy, and everything that is bought is a variation on one of these themes or to satisfy one of the following needs:

- Shelter, which includes clothing;
- Food, including drink;
- Sex and reproductive success; and
- Relational safety.

Probably, neither now nor in the foreseeable future will law corporations or firms be in the business of selling housing, clothing, food or beverages, or sex. The business that lawyers are, and have always been in, is the same one that psychologists, doctors, priests, parents, tarot-card readers, accountants, and insurance salespeople (among many, many others) are in. They are catering to the strongest of all human needs: the need for relational safety.

It's a fundamental fact about humans that we seek safety within relationships. Recent research has shown that almost all our actions are related to our drive to form or consolidate relationships with those who we believe will support us. Our greatest fear is of abandonment.

All those pieces of the legal business which are not germane to establishing supportive relationships are the ones which are being, and are increasingly in danger of being, disaggregated. What will be left is the factor which is most saleable: the relationship between the partner – or whatever they might be called in 10–15 years – and the client.

While that relationship provides safety and support, it is a valuable service. The Big 4 realized this some time ago and began to expand out of accountancy and concentrate on what they call "advisory", which in PwC's case – besides the normal accountancy services – includes strategy, performance enhancement, legal services, deal-making, sustainability, and climate change etc. It's all about relationship safety. It's about entering into their "tribe" and letting them look after you. It's a hard act to follow.

Ask yourself what you are really in business for.

What will law leaders do?

But this quest for relationships is not only the future of law firm sales, business development, and marketing, it's also the future of law firm management. Much of the work that managing partners do today will also be decomposed. Break down almost any task – even one that seems so very important that only the top person can do it – and a machine can do it better, or it can be outsourced to some enterprise who can do it better and certainly cheaper.

If we look at leadership through a neurogenetic lens, we find that people follow leaders because they believe that person will make them safe. If employees, or partners, feel that the managing partner, or CEO, has their back, has their interests at heart, and has a clear vision of how to deliver them from perceived threats, then they will become committed to them and, through that commitment, will be more engaged with the business. They will also become more productive, for a whole variety of reasons which we will go into later.

The law firm leader will also "lead" far fewer people. The race to the bottom in terms of the numbers employed has only just begun in professional service firms. In many legal businesses non-legal support staff have already been all-but eliminated. Paradoxically, this will necessitate the managing partner, or CEO, having even greater people skills and being able to engender even greater commitment.

Conclusion

Very few lawyers presently in law firms have the right traits and skills for the future. There are too many specialists, too many black-letter lawyers, and too many legal technicians. Few of these will be needed in the firm of the future. What will be needed will be men and women who understand the art of listening, questioning, and giving advice in a way that gives clients a sense of safety. These people will understand business and, more importantly, the psychology of running and operating a business. They will be more like advisory partners in the Big 4.

Such people are rare in law firms at present and there will be great competition for them in the future. The law leader of the future will need to be able to interact with these people in ways that are quite different from the present. The science of human behavior shows how a leader can retain, inspire, and motivate this new class of "lawyer" (and we will explore this further in the next chapter of this book).

In fact, behavioral science comes into play in every aspect of running a legal business, from the way we make decisions, to the way we deliver good or bad news, interrelate with clients, and communicate. You don't have to be a scientist to use the tools derived from this new knowledge, you just have to follow the tips outlined in each of the following chapters. If you do, you will have a first-rate, successful business – and you won't even worry too much about whether it's a law business or not.

Chapter 2:
The human science of strategy

This chapter will:

- Look at what strategic thinking really is;
- Ask who does best at it; and
- Propose a "how to" for making strategic initiatives work.

The character of competition between law firms has changed over the last 10 or so years. Turbulence has increased in terms of the leaders and the laggards. It is harder and harder to stay on top, or even to maintain your position in the second or third tier of firms. Research by MIT has found that those firms that win tend to win bigger than ever before. They get bigger market shares and the gap in profitability between the top and the bottom is larger than it was before.

Every firm needs to evolve a strategy to cope with this new reality. Leaders need to realize that any strategy they come up with may only be valid for a year, or even just six months. It's a game that never ends.

Law firm strategy

Strategy was long seen as an art form rather than a science. There were "hunches" and "gut feelings" and those who were "market savvy". Then there were elaborate models and processes, all of which were supposed to project to the future rather than the past. More recently, the advent of mega data has fooled many law firm leaders into thinking that all that was needed was to reach into the honeypot of data, hire a "strategy" consultant who will apply an algorithm to analyze that data and, on the basis of it, predict future trends. Bingo! Up will come a scientifically sound strategy for the firm. That strategy will probably be the same, or very similar, to the one that the consultancy has devised for a dozen other firms, and probably the same, or very much akin, to the strategies devised for other firms by other consultants. Especially since they are all using essentially the same algorithms and the same mega data.

There are many reasons for this. An algorithm will not tell you which way the market is heading, or how you ought to respond. It will tell you what is going on now, and reveal the factors that led to that being the case. One of the greatest mistakes in decision making is to assume that the future will be like the past. As chaos theory has shown, it almost inevitably won't. The mega data and the algorithm tell you about the past and the present, not the future. Those mathematical models are an important part of the strategy determination process. What is left out are the sciences, such as behavioral neurogenetics, which show what human beings are all about.

Despite all the algorithms, all the mathematical models, only a very few economists – most famously, Stern Business School's Professor Nouriel Roubini – predicted the crash of 2008. What was ignored by the rest of the financial strategists can be summed up in a quote from Pablo Picasso: "Computers are useless; all they give you is answers." The answers are indeed useless if the questions that are fed into the computers are wrong. The planners, government and private, saw an upward trend, based on what was working then.

Strategy is about asking the right questions, without which the "right" answers are useless. In our experience, law leaders – like many of their corporate fellows – are less than perfect at asking questions. For example, one large national law firm fell sharply from its premier position in spite of putting in place many initiatives that should have helped. Guided by a major global consultancy, they reorganized internally to ensure that practice group leaders would have strong touch points with all partners. They put in place a leading-edge (on paper) program to retain and develop good lawyers. They brought in speakers on innovation and planned for money-saving, activity-based workplaces at all their locations. They did not ask – or certainly respond adequately to – two basic questions. One: What do clients really want of us? (The answers would probably have been faster responses and coming up with suggestions on broader problems to the ones they were hired for.) Two: How do we build trust at all levels of the organization? (Without this there could be little effective mentoring or motivation to change, or indeed to stay in the firm.)

What is "strategic thought"?

There are many, many definitions of strategic thought, most of which make perfectly good common sense. To a law leader, they are very enticing, and almost all firms have in some way tried to incorporate strategic thinking into their firms. However, in many ways science is throwing a spanner into the works and saying that strategic thinking is not what it seems to be.

The current, widely accepted, model of strategic thinking involves, among other things[1]:

- A "focused intent", which means being more determined and less distracted than rivals in the market place.

- Being "hypothesis driven" ensuring that both creative and critical thinking are incorporated into strategy making. This competency supposedly explicitly incorporates the scientific method into strategic thinking.[2]

- Having "intelligent opportunism", which means being responsive to good opportunities.

These three mental processes require a number of what psychologists would call "executive" cognitive actions. These include decision making, short and long-term memory recall, knowing and challenging conscious and unconscious assumptions and beliefs, focusing, and so forth. Pretty "heady" stuff, it would seem.

Perhaps not, however. According to the latest research, all these activities or characteristics may not be under our conscious "cognitive" control at all. Instead, they are the result of other, less recognized, biological processes. Our "strategic thinking" is, in fact, determined by our genes, our experiences, our emotions, and our neurochemical and neurophysiological make-up. Not to mention the actions and reactions of the other major "brains" that humans – like all animals – have, including those of our gut, heart, and skin. Every second that passes, all of these are feeding information into the decision centers of the "head brain", which remains totally unaware of the process. The brains of the heart, the gut, and the skin remember and process experience and collaborate with the orbitofrontal cortex and other parts of the head brain to form unconscious assumptions and beliefs which will be acted on automatically when certain triggers occur.

In terms of decisions – for example, being responsive to opportunities – most modern research shows that we don't make rational decisions in the way people have historically thought we do. We don't think, "Ah, this is an opportunity, I had better take it". In fact, by the time we have thought this, the decision to act or not has been taken. By that time, the mind (a term we use to include the sum of all of the various elements in our neurogenetic make-up) has very quickly gone through a number of unconscious calculations in answer to a number of fundamental questions. These include:

- How will this affect the nexus of my supportive relationships or those I want to include in that nexus?
- Will taking this opportunity make me more, or less, safe?
- Would the actions involved in seizing this opportunity expose me to any loss or social exclusion?
- Would taking this opportunity gain me status in the eyes of those I care about?
- What is the level of certainty regarding this?
- Will this increase or decrease the amount of control that I have over my life?
- What do I feel about this decision?

The conscious brain doesn't answer these questions; no "thinking" takes place. The "answers" are automatic and based on genetics and experiential memories of the various brains. For example, the very act of recognizing an opportunity in the first place is genetically based. It involves the same genetic factors which make a person either open or not to new experience.[3] You can train someone who has that genetic propensity to be better at it, but you can't expect someone who doesn't have that genetic expression to be able to "recognize an opportunity", far less to act on it.

Science is very quickly coming to the conclusion that "strategic thinking", as a conscious activity which a person can put their mind to, may be like the yeti of the Himalayas: a myth. There are aspects of it which some people may be better at, because of their genes and their experience, but probably nobody will be good at all of the mental abilities that are attributed to the "strategic thinker". Pity, but there it is.

Science shows us that, in terms of "strategic thought", gut wins over process every time.

Who is the best strategist?

So, who is the best strategist? Who do you rely on for strategic advice, counsel, and guidance? Surprisingly, the answer is: on yourself, in conjunction with a team of diverse individuals. There are many reasons for this, which we will examine. However, there are also many competing candidates for the position. Among these are the large strategy houses – the Bains, BCGs, and McKinseys of this world – artificial intelligence, and the game theorists. Or a combination of all of the above.

The dominant strategy consultancies with their big data and complex algorithms are not necessarily the answer. A number of people, such as Walter Kiechel in his now-famous book, *Lords of Strategy*, claim that statistically the majority of their suggestions end in expensive failure.[4] Many CEOs and others rely on these organizations because they were trained by them. In fact, 70 percent of present and past Fortune 500 corporation CEOs are McKinsey alumni.[5]

Strategy is often said to be about "game theory". This is a field that examines how individuals devise the best strategy based on their opponents' moves in a competitive situation. It's a principle found in many aspects of daily life, from government to business to sports. When a soccer player decides at what angle to take a penalty kick by anticipating the goalie's response, or a person tries to negotiate a job offer with their boss, these individuals' actions are explained by reference to game theory. It assumes two or more rational players. It involves prediction through pattern recognition and short-term memory.

Sounds good. As you may recall the ex-finance minister of Greece, Yanis Varoufakis, is an expert on game theory and has written a book and numerous papers on the subject. However, his failure in the bail-out talks of 2015 might give one pause before relying too heavily on his, or any other game-theorist's, advice on the future of your firm.

In fact, if you're looking for the right person to use game theory for strategic guidance, you may not be looking at the right species at all. Better to go to the local zoological gardens, and meet Mr (or Ms) strategy themselves: the chimpanzee.

A 2014 study published in the journal *Nature* demonstrated that chimps are much better at game theory, and thus strategy, in the sense that game theorists understand it, than humans.[6] They have a far greater ability for pattern recognition and considerably superior short-term memory. They are better able to predict a rival's move – even in a game that they've just been taught – than a human opponent. This is because game theory assumes that all players of the game – or devisers of strategy

– are acting rationally. The simple fact is that humans are much less rational than other animals, including chimps. In the study, the chimps beat their human opponents so resoundingly that they came close to the theoretical maximum number of times you can win at the games.

A chimp's, or almost any other sentient animal's, actions are far more likely to be based on reason and facts than a human's (due to the different make-up of their brains' limbic system and frontal cortex). Further, game theory assumes that humans will act competitively. It's not in our genes to be as competitive as a chimpanzee. We are, like our near cousins the bonobos, overwhelmingly a cooperative species. Since we do better when we act in line with our genetics, then it would follow that a more cooperative and non-rational approach to strategy would be better than relying on game theory. And so it turns out in practice.

If chimpanzees are a bit too animalistic for you, why not leave strategy to artificial intelligence? There's an increasingly good argument for this, especially if you believe that data is the answer to everything. AI works on the basis of analyzing data, as do many executive functions. Most of the jobs that lawyers and law firm leaders do involves analyzing data – whether it's going through boxes full of discovery papers to decide which ones are relevant or deciding whom to appoint to a particular position. In the latter case, the prospect's employment past, their social and scholastic background, their achievements, the clubs they belong to and so forth are all data you take into account when selecting whom to interview. Both of these jobs are now routinely done by machines.

There's a quote that we love from the data scientist Jeremy Howard: "It is certainly not the case that domain expertise (law, running a firm, managing) is suddenly redundant. But data expertise is at least as important and will become exponentially more important. So this is the trick. Data will tell you what's really going on, whereas domain expertise will always bias you towards the status quo."[7] Good, so far – we don't want the status quo.

But there's a limitation. Picasso's quip, quoted above, comes to mind. It's not that AI and computers are useless, far from it. They're essential – as is the data they analyze. But answers are always the result of questions. Properly handled, the data will lead you to questions – like the data on a CV.

The facts presented should lead to questions such as: "How well will this candidate fit in with the culture of the firm?", "Does his history show a level of curiosity?", or "Is she adept at making friends, is she an influencer?" Oddly enough, in our experience, these more EQ or SQ (emotional intelligence or social intelligence) questions are hardly ever asked. In terms of the process of developing a good strategy, arriving at answers is the least important part of it. And arriving at questions is not something that machines, or game theory, are good at.

So, as we said earlier, the best person to develop the firm's strategy is you, in conjunction with a team of the most diverse of your colleagues. Your job, as a team, is to come up with the right questions. To achieve this, you and your team have to challenge your own and each other's assumptions. This can be a hard process because, as much recent research has shown, people don't like their assumptions being challenged, particularly a "truth" on which their career has been based. Your cherished assumptions and beliefs can become part of your personality, part of the core of you. We have seen law leaders martyr themselves, their careers, and their firms' future rather than admit they were wrong. Yet research from Harvard and other universities has shown that up to 90 percent of all our assumptions are mistaken.

The other problem with assumptions is that maybe half of them are unconscious. We simply don't know we have them. A really good leader will analyze all their past decisions and actions to see what hidden assumptions may be at play. This is best done in the company of someone you trust who has a different background.

A strategy group that is not diverse enough may also share any number of hidden assumptions. Many of these are the result of similar backgrounds and experience – the same social class, the same schools, the same nationality, the same religion, similar experiences, and training in the same kinds of firms. All of these predispose us to think in the same way and force us to adopt, quite unconsciously in early childhood or later, a similar set of assumptions and beliefs. Group think, like those McKinsey alumnae.

This is one of the reasons why so much research has shown that diverse groups make the best decisions – they don't share a whole lot of unconscious assumptions. And, if there's enough relational safety, they're more ready to challenge the assumptions of other members of the group. Any questions that you come up with must be free of these road blocks to clarity.

So, how do you identify the right questions?

Beware of formulaic or obvious questions. For example "Where will the market (economy) go in the next five years?" – it sounds so good and so obvious. It's a pre-2008 question, which is why they all got it wrong.

We've heard law leaders say that they can't plan if they don't know the answer to that question. We reply that whatever answer you get will almost certainly be wrong.

Often, one question begets another, which in turn leads to a deeper question:

"Where do we want to be in five years?"

"Who is 'we?'"

"OK. As leader, where do I want the firm to be in five years' time?"

"Really? Me or the firm?"

We are beginning, here, to get to the nub of many firms' problems: the leader confusing their own aims and ambitions with those of the firm. Most corporate and firm mergers fail because the CEOs or the managing partners have entered into them as a way of enhancing their own egos or reputations. Often, this is not intentional, but is the result of a fundamental human driver – the need to increase one's status. Leading a bigger firm or corporation does just that. In a sense, the managing partner or even a potential managing partner is the very last person you should rely on to provide the firm's direction.

When you have decided what the right questions are, then and only then should you consult analytics to get their algorithms working on the big data. Another danger that hidden assumptions pose arises when the answers to the questions come in. There will always be a selection of answers to any given question. In choosing an answer, you need to ensure that you are not blinded by assumptions or desires that are not relevant to the issue. And yet each individual is neurobiologically "programmed" to do this. Again, it is you and the diverse group who must go over the answers and decide which ones to explore further.

So, the answer to the question of who does strategy best is you, the law leader, in conjunction with a diverse group of people – probably not just the members of your current C-suite who may well have the same worldview and set of hidden assumptions that you have.

TOP TIP

Go over your past actions and decisions and find your own hidden assumptions, perhaps with the help of a trusted person with a different view point. You may be surprised by the result. If you're not, you didn't do it right.

How to make strategic initiatives work

The tragic truth is that, as research has shown, up to 90 percent of all strategic initiatives fail to achieve the results expected of them. Particularly the financial results. We don't want to go into all the reasons for this failure rate, most of which have nothing to do with the strategy itself.

A successful strategy is only successful because it has been successfully implemented. About 70 percent of that 90 percent is due to implementation failure.[8] There are a number of factors which contribute to making a good strategy successful. We call them the "Magnificent Seven" of implementation:

1. A management style at all levels of the firm that is appropriate to change;

2. Leadership devoting sufficient time to the implementation process;

3. Sufficient trust at all levels of the firm;

4. An aligned culture;

5. A vision that makes sense to the whole firm, and to clients;

6. A sense of mutual support throughout the firm; and

7. The involvement of all of the firm in the process.

Most of these we will be dealing with in some detail later in the book. Here, we'd like to concentrate on the second, fifth, and sixth of these prerequisites for success, namely:

- The need for leadership to maintain focus on the implementation process;

- The need to convince all stakeholders – partners, lawyers, support staff, and present and potential clients – of the reason for the strategy; and

- A feeling by everyone in the firm that they belong to a mutually supportive "tribe".

Maintaining long-term focus

This isn't easy for any leader – especially the leader of a large firm. There are reports for the board, meetings, day-to-day emergencies, press interviews, and so on. Often, these come as a relief from the more arduous job of managing long-term strategic change.

Two short case studies:

One large law firm we were called in to help had developed a perfectly good remuneration strategy. With the help of consultants, they had asked all the right questions, engaged the partners, and come up with a solution that everyone, including us, thought would work. However, it failed to achieve its objectives of increasing both the engagement of the partners and raising their productivity in terms of new business.

It turned out that the managing partner was, at that time, preoccupied with things related neither to this initiative or to the firm and left the application of the initiative to the practice leaders, who in turn had other things on their minds – including which of them would succeed the managing partner (none of them did; he chose to remain).

In another large firm, the merger with an overseas partner was rendered practically meaningless by the neglect of both the overseas and the local managing partners. This neglect was largely caused by the arrival of the crash of 2008/9, which forced the leaders to shift their focus onto other things more immediately related to their individual firm's survival.

The neglect of one aspect of the business to concentrate on another is largely a result of our neurogenetics. Humans are not programmed to be good at multitasking. Recent research has shown that women are somewhat better at it than men (the MPs mentioned in the two examples above were all male). This is because, in ancient times when our genome was developing, gathering with young children in tow required a multi focus. Hunting, on the other hand, mostly but not always the domain of men, required far more of an undivided focus because the danger that the activity involved came mostly from their prey.

Another genetic pitfall is that the MAOA gene, which regulates focus, comes in two varieties: a long and a short form. If you've got one form of the gene you are able to concentrate on the detail of what you're doing, and if you have the other your mind tends to wander and you neglect the detail. More people have the latter configuration, and that unfortunately includes law leaders.

The solution is for the leader to know and acknowledge what they are good at, and be aware of the attention-giving abilities of those around them. That way, the various tasks can be handled by the right people who can give them sufficient attention. This avoids the fatal "this, too, will pass" attitude which can develop among staff and partners when management no longer seems interested in the initiative.

One of the most difficult strategic initiatives to implement is the merger between two large firms. Few have succeeded adequately. One of those few was the merger between the Australian firm Freehills and the UK firm Herbert Smith. The merger was led by Mark Rigotti and Sonya Leydecker, who became the joint CEOs of the new firm. They saw the danger that could come from their and other leaders' attention being diverted from the integration of the two firms by more immediate concerns.

"We set up a separate integration office", Rigotti told us. "It was apart from the main business and populated with people who left behind their 'day jobs' and focused just on integration. This dealt with a lot of the 'plumbing', which allowed the partners, other fee earners, and the various support functions like business development to focus on connecting and collaborating effectively to win work and service clients. That integration office unlocked a number of procurement benefits which more than covered its cost and allowed us to fast-track a number of things. This gave us momentum. It was a key implementation driver."

If you don't have the time to stay on top of the implementation of strategy, you're the wrong person to lead it!

Convincing stakeholders that the strategy has a purpose, a vision – beyond the self-aggrandizement of the firm leadership – and communicating (in a way that gets buy-in) the link between the vision and the strategy is vital to the success of any initiative. Rigotti puts it this way: "A vision states what you want to be. A strategy is how you get there. It follows that you need a compelling vision that the organization and its people can coalesce around." For a number of reasons which we'll look at later, few visions are particularly compelling.

Communication about a new strategy and its implementation is about listening and reacting to concerns as much as outlining what the strategy is. Unfortunately, in our experience, communication is usually a one-way street. This inevitably leads to disengagement and failure.

Wherever possible, the discussion about the need for a new strategy should be face to face and in small groups. We are hard-wired to trust face-to-face communication far more than any other medium.

Professor Robin Dunbar and his team at Oxford University have shown that humans are only capable of relating to about 150 people.[9] Beyond that number (and that includes Facebook friends), he maintains that we cease to think of humans as individuals, and cease to care in a mutually supportive sense.

Communicating in person to small groups is also important. Humans are small group animals. Successful communication is closely tied in with group size. Humans need to feel special, to feel individually important because, in ancient times, that specialness was the key to getting the support needed to survive. That's why we each strive for status. Communicating en masse to large groups deprives them of that sense of status and can even turn them against you and your strategy. Of course, you as a law leader may not be able to sit in person with all the members of your firm. Other levels of management – and influencers – will sometimes have to do this for you, once they have become convinced of the strategy and the implementation of it.

This sense of needing to be special affects what you communicate about the strategy as well. In a large firm, strategies that are communicated as being "in the best interests of the firm" will cut little ice with anybody except the leadership. To be blunt, no member of the firm outside those at the very top really cares about the organization. They care about themselves, their families, their team, their clients, and their close friends. Yet, for the most part, strategic initiatives are communicated in terms of the firm, and this communication is done either electronically or in large meetings. All too often, the result is antagonism, eye-roll, and failure.

Bob (one of the authors) lived with hunter-gatherers for about a year in the Kalahari in southern Africa. He watched how they decided on and communicated strategic decisions. To these people, a strategic decision might have been choosing a new hunting ground, foraging for mollusks rather than hunting gnu, or establishing barter discussions with another, unrelated, group. Modern strategic decisions may be more complex, but they are, essentially, of the same ilk.

First, the council of elders came up with a series of options, usually favoring one or more of them. They would then gather the whole of the band over the age of six – in this case 53 in all – and they would put the case for those options they favored. There would often follow a spirited debate. No final decision would be taken until all of those present agreed – no matter how long it took. The same sort of behavior has been observed by other researchers in hunter-gatherer bands in the Congo, in South America, and among Australian Aborigines (in the early 20th century when there were still Aboriginal Australians living the hunting and gathering lifestyle).[10]

This is how we humans made strategic decisions for perhaps two or more million years. Any action or behavior with that sort of pedigree becomes part of our genetic propensity and, as such, allows us to operate within our design specs. Our autonomy is intact, we get less stressed, more accepting, and the strategy is more successfully implemented.

But we're not hunter-gatherers, and we largely operate in multinational firms of well over 150 people. So, what are the practical take-aways we can glean from our genetics? What should law leaders actually do to give them the greatest chance of success?

1. Frame the strategy in terms that are meaningful to individuals. Individuals make decisions, even in a group context.

2. Communicate the strategy in terms of options, not dictats.

3. Communicate it face-to-face to small groups.

4. Allow argument and debate, and be prepared to defend your favored option.

5. Be prepared to vary, or alter, the strategy – after all, you'll only know if it is the right one in retrospect, and statistically 70 percent of all decisions are wrong.[11]

6. Make sure that your strategy stems from an emotionally strong and meaningful purpose.

Foster an atmosphere of mutual support

Much research has been carried out about why people come to work, and stay working, for an organization. Money is, of course, important, but taken by itself, is only number 13 in the list of reasons. More important – in fact, on top of the list – are relationships. As relationship-forming animals, we come to work to be with a "tribe", a nexus of people with whom we have things in common and from whom we derive support. If we don't find we have mutually supportive or satisfactory relationships, we leave when we can.

This human need for supportive relationships is crucial in all areas of law firm management. Used well, it can improve engagement and productivity, enhance business development, or make the implementation of a strategy a success. And mutually supportive means just that:

the partners, the support staff, the junior lawyers must all feel that they will mutually gain by the change in direction, that they are part of the reason for the initiative.

Of course, the start of the strategy formulation and implementation process is much too late to begin to create an atmosphere of mutual trust and support. That needs to be an ongoing effort by leadership. A firm is not just a business, it is a tribe, and it's the modern equivalent of a hunter-gatherer band. Without that sense of mutuality, any change initiative is doomed to failure because the human genome is designed so that we give support only to those we feel will support us.

"The big lesson is that success depends on people", reflects Michael Rose, the managing partner of Allens Linklaters. "If people know each other, respect each other's capabilities, and trust each other, they will work effectively together and clients will notice. This personal chemistry is critical to success, regardless of structure."

From what they tell us, partners in many larger firms feel that they have little real say in the running of "their" firm. This loss of a sense of ownership – belonging – is a dangerous impediment to successful strategy implementation. This is something that law leaders will have to urgently address if they want their firms to survive the "new normal".

Start forming a culture of mutual trust and support as soon as you become a leader.

Conclusion

In essence, any strategy is only a way of ensuring that the tribe survives, whether that is going from gnu to mollusks or becoming a virtual rather than a physical law firm. This means that the implementation of that strategy must, as Michael Rose says, be about people.

For success you need:

- The combination of human science and technology. Don't just rely on the machines or the data, focus on how human beings really work.

- A strategy that is based on a vision which all of the stakeholders can accept. This also means communicating it to them in human terms.

- To concentrate on asking the right questions rather than finding the right answers.

- An aligned culture. (More on this later.)

- Total commitment on the part of the leadership. This must be seen to be the case by all stakeholders.

- A style of leadership appropriate to the change process. (More on this later.)

- A high level of trust at all levels of the firm. (Again, more on this later.)

- Flexibility and a willingness to change. This means allowing for the fact that other people may have better ideas than you do.

- A keen awareness of the danger of group think. Don't just talk to those who share your background. In many ways, these people can be the worst enemies of strategy and its implementation.

- Above all, trust yourself. You need enough trust in yourself to challenge your own motivations and assumptions, and to seek the help you must have to ferret out those assumptions that are hidden from your consciousness.

References

1. Liedtka, J., "Linking Strategic Thinking with Strategic Planning", *Strategy and Leadership*, 26(4), 30-35, 1998.
2. Liedtka, J., "Strategic Thinking—can it be taught?" *Long Range Planning*, 31(1), 120-129, 1998.
3. Shane, S. et al, "Do openness to experience and recognizing opportunities have the same genetic source?" *Human Resource Management*, 40(2), 291-303, 2010.
4. Kiechel, W., *Lords of Strategy*, Harvard Business Press, Boston MA, 2010.
5. McDonald, D., *The Firm: The Story of McKinsey and Its Secret Influence on American Business*, Simon & Shuster, New York, 2013.
6. Flynn Martin, C. et al, *Scientific Reports*, 4 (5182), 2014; available at www.nature.com/articles/srep05182.
7. Interview in McKinsey Quarterly, September 2014; available at www.mckinsey.com/insights/strategy/artificial_intelligence_meets_the_c-suite.
8. Bass, B., "Executive and strategic leadership" International Journal Of Business, 12(1), 33-53, 2007.
9. Dunbar, R., *Lucy to Language*, OUP, Oxford, 2014.
10. O'Hara, P., *Encyclopaedia of Political Economy*, Routledge, London, 2002.
11. Heath, C. and D., *Decisive*, Crown Business, Danvers MA, 2013.

Chapter 3:
Leading the organization of the future

In this chapter we cover:

- What leadership means to humans;
- What styles of leadership are best for different situations, including the constant change we find ourselves in today;
- What science can tell us about what makes a good, or even great, leader; and
- Leadership in the law environment.

When we think of leadership today, whether in business or politics, one of our favorite poems, W. B. Yeats' "The Second Coming", comes to mind:

"Turning and turning in the widening gyre
The falcon cannot hear the falconer
Things fall apart; the centre cannot hold
Mere anarchy is loosed upon the world."

In today's uncertain and constantly changing work and social environment, many professional services firms seem to be without direction; they are wallowing in high seas and, to continue the sailing metaphor, the sails cannot catch the fickle wind. People in law, as elsewhere, are uneasy about the future of their practice, firm, the profession of law, and even, in many cases, the future of work as done by human beings.

Huge and unrealistic expectations are placed on leaders, often resulting in disappointment. This in turn can lead to the perception that, as in Yeats' poem, "the centre cannot hold"; trust in leadership is lost and people doubt or cannot even clearly hear the leaders' messages. Unity falls apart, cooperation diminishes or vanishes. Even where clear strategies are communicated, there may be no agreement or fully effective implementation.

What kind of leadership is needed in such times? The leader – actually leaders – must form a strong, united, and mutually complementary core. This stable center holds the firm securely in its gravitational field and cascades down to all levels of the firm. Leaders provide a compelling vision and gain commitment from their people and, in the context of that trust and emotional safety, from each other. This network of committed relationships forms a reliable relational environment which consistently stimulates and enables vital neurogenic drivers to do their job. In this safe and sure context, people can withstand and even thrive amid ongoing fluctuations and change.

CASE STUDY

We work in an advisory capacity for government agencies as well as multinational corporations and firms. One government agency leader we encountered described the extreme challenges of his team, which deals with global security issues. His direct reports are mostly young, exceptionally talented, and highly qualified. Their work life involves minimal certainty; frequent disruption, and constant travel, often to new destinations, usually at little or no notice; long and unpredictable hours; and frequent danger. Often, they are asked to immediately change roles and priorities as an urgent need crops up. Yet they handle these extreme stressors and remain motivated and committed, and for the most part they enjoy their work. There is a long waiting list to join his team. "How does this happen?", we asked.

"We have a strong leadership center, consisting of myself and a few of my top people", he explained. "We rely totally on each other. No matter where we all are in the world, we check in at least daily, whenever possible for face-to-face conversations, admittedly electronic. I not only want to know their conclusions, but also to watch their faces while they walk me through their thinking process, especially if their view is different to mine, in which case I am ready to change my opinion. We are all constantly learning new things. If a mistake is made, they know I will go to the wall for them and back them completely. I'm extremely protective of them, their safety, and their wellbeing. And they, in turn, bring that total dedication to those who report to them."

With all that's been written about what makes good leadership, you would have to go far to find a better description than the example cited in the case study above. But let's break those elements down and understand more deeply why they work and how to achieve them.

What leadership means to humans

Leadership as we know it today is not natural to human beings, which may help to explain why there are so few good leaders. Except in times of crisis, hunter-gatherer tribes did not have single leaders.[1] There were people whose abilities or interest may have led them to take a primary role in certain activities, from hunting to spiritual rituals, but on the whole overall "leadership" was discouraged. When conflicts did arise, perhaps involving competition over mates or relationship squabbles, the elders were trusted to help settle them. Becoming an elder was not a matter of politicking or amassing a fortune, but simply living until about the age of 35.[2]

When Alicia was trekking in the Afghan mountains as a very young woman, she came across a tiny village of stone huts built into the side of a mountain. The villagers had never seen a European before. She and her companions asked, through one of their guides who spoke some English, who the leader was. After much discussion between the guide and several villagers, the answer finally came back. There was a man whom people looked to for questions about their flock and growing corn, and one who took the lead on matters involving contact with other villages and, in very rare cases, the large town on the faraway plains. While these people were herders and farmers more than roaming hunter-gatherers, this gives an idea of how unfamiliar our concept of leadership is to those not used to it.

Leadership styles

Returning to hunter-gatherers, in extreme cases, such as when facing natural disasters or when a band got too big and had to split up, individual hunter-gatherers did arise who insisted on certain actions and influenced others to follow. For example: "We need to cross this rapid-flowing river to get to the other side. You trust me, and I am certain we can do this. Yes, there are crocodiles and water snakes, but we must cross. Now."[3]

The woman or man urging the band to take the risk of crossing the river is showing a leadership style often referred to as "transactional" or "authoritarian". It's a kind of "just do it" approach, and it has its place in a one-off crisis. If the leader is trusted, people will turn to them for guidance and take certain actions at the time. It is not the style for sustainable change, or for innovation.

Another style is known as "laissez-faire". The laissez-faire leader largely looks after their people by letting them get on with it, and if necessary making sure they have the resources they need and running interference. This works well with very high-performing teams who are experts at what they do and who may have more specific knowledge or expertise than any one manager. In fact, leadership is often shared among team members, with perhaps certain people taking the lead on specific tasks or when their own area of expertise is a general priority.

The best – in reality the only effective – leadership style in times when ongoing change and innovation are needed, or when the firm adopts ambitious goals and growth targets, is what's called "transformational leadership". The transformational leader is affiliative, stimulates discussion and debate, and above all encourages their people to learn, grow, experiment, and develop. This is a very facilitative and coaching style, although the leader does not shirk from making final decisions and taking responsibility for their outcome.[4]

The transformational leader and their executive communicate a clear direction and expectations, giving both authority and accountability for agreed outcomes. With the leader's support and oversight, people feel safe enough to make sustainable behavioral change, try new approaches, and innovate.

Transformational leadership is predominantly a female style.[5] However, men can become great transformational leaders. Perhaps the greatest of all American CEOs of the 20th Century, Lee Iacocca, was both male and transformational in his management style.[6]

Attributes and capabilities of a good leader
Engenders commitment
More than anything, being a great leader requires the ability to get others invested in the relationship with you. As does almost everything, this of course harks back to the fact that humans are relationship-forming creatures and that 80 percent of our neurobiology and genetics are geared simply to surround ourselves with a nexus of supportive relationships.[7] If people feel that they have a strong real – or even a potential – relationship with you, their neurogenetic system will self-organize to follow your lead in order to strengthen that relationship. As we show in Chapter 8, they will be very disposed to take on your ideas.

This is true even if your propositions are illogical, lack evidence, or even fly in the face of all known facts. Which, of course, goes a long way towards explaining the mass suicide in Georgetown, suicide bombers now, and the Einsatzgruppen during WW2. It is the reason demagogues come to power and sway people to take positions they would not otherwise adopt and actions it would be better if they didn't. On the flip side, it is also how great leaders such as Churchill inspired people to overcome their fears, make great sacrifices, and defeat a common enemy.

It is also true that leaders are galvanized by their followers, who become their perceived support network. This is why many politicians will do almost anything to retain power; the fear of losing that support nexus is too strong.

On the other hand, great leaders will develop a strong protectiveness towards their people and, like a parent, a fierce desire for their well-being. Every healthy parent knows the protectiveness that sets in with the birth of a child, the overpowering drive to ensure its safety and well-being. In functional leaders, a similar transformation takes place when they are put in a position of responsibility for people.[8]

One very good leader of a global law firm that we know and esteem was loved and admired by his firm, which he led for nearly a decade. He was seen as caring, fair, available, and when necessary tough. Even those who felt his decisions went against their personal interests respected him. People felt they could call him if they had a problem and he would take care of it or ensure it was dealt with appropriately.

This man brought the firm to a position of prominence and financial strength and shepherded it through a very difficult and ambitious global merger with unanimous support from his home firm, something that is rare in such cases. The negotiations were stressful and tough. Just at the peak of his triumph he suffered a near-fatal stroke. He survived and, shortly after, at the end of his long and successful tenure, left the firm in the hands of a well-prepared successor. In spite of the opinion of his doctors, many of his people did not see his stroke as a coincidence; they felt he had literally given his all for them.

Not all leaders, of course, feel this intense loyalty to (or from) their organization or firm. Many of today's corporate CEOs are vastly overpaid and their innate need for supportive relationships has been twisted into an insatiable thirst for personal recognition or fame and the trappings of status at the cost of their people, customers, and shareholders. The paradox is that leaders who are not truly committed to their organizations will never engender the support of someone who is.

Affiliative

As we have seen, human beings are genetically geared for single leadership only under certain conditions. These are principally in times of perceived danger, when people feel under attack by forces over which they have no control. Today, with our ever-growing sense of uncertainty and fear, people often feel the need for a parental figure to somehow put things right. This places a great stress on today's leaders.

The uncertainty tends to throw up leaders who are seen as "strong", but not particularly transformational. Hence, perhaps, the "imperial CEO". Even law firms have their share of them. The best leadership structure is one in which strong, united groups of leaders such as a board and executive work closely and constructively together.[9]

In a firm, the job of the board chair, managing partner, or CEO is to facilitate the unity and joint-decision-making capability within the group, largely through nurturing a sense of mutual respect and commitment. The managing partner or CEO is also responsible for their executive members' performance and development in their line areas, and for ensuring that the vision, strategy, and desired culture are agreed and embedded throughout the organization.

This requires an exceptionally affiliative style and the capability to engender commitment in people, unite them under the leader's relationship canopy, and bring out the best in groups and individuals. The affiliative leader enjoys working with people and is stimulated by the exchange of ideas and emotions. They can put aside their own preconceptions long enough to hear the opinions of others and facilitate genuinely generative conversations in which individuals or groups come to new insights and ideas through the exchange.[10]

Behaves with empathy and resonance

Much has been written about the need for a "resonant" leader, one who is high in emotional, or better yet, social intelligence: who has empathy and awareness of self and others. Like all other relationship attributes, this ability emanates from the brain's limbic system, which governs trust, safety, and decision making. It is largely essential for a coaching style of leadership.

Empathy is driven by a network of what are called "mirror cells". This unconscious system stimulates us to directly feel what we perceive others feel. An empathetic leader is often able to know others' emotions by tuning in to their own. This can be a bit tricky because often we assume that what we are feeling reflects what others are experiencing, when in fact it does not. Accurately assessing what's going on for others requires the self-knowledge to recognize whether the emotion is generated internally – perhaps because it is one of your usual emotional patterns – or is more likely strongly influenced by someone else's experience. It also requires consciously using all your senses to observe signals from the other person – such as shining eyes on the verge of crying, the quivering of lips around the mouth, change in breathing patterns, an alteration in posture, clenching of muscles, or a change in tone of voice.

While empathy is a definite plus for a leader, it must be managed with awareness. Like sympathy, it can be wrongly used or over-used. There is a time for sitting with someone and commiserating, but in the end, the most reliable tool for a leader is showing real and appropriate curiosity about people, and tuning in fully – using all the senses – to what they say.

Resonance is a specific aspect of relationship, related to empathy. This is driven by spindle cells, which allow leaders to quickly choose the best way to respond to someone; and oscillators, which synchronize people's physical movements. Examples of the latter are people falling into step, orchestras playing in harmony, and people coming to the same conclusion at the same time. When a group of people share the same "frequency" they experience a strong sense of safety and unison. Great leaders are those whose behaviors powerfully leverage this complex system of brain interconnectedness.[11] A "resonant" leader is in tune with their people in a very literal sense.

Able to trust and be trusted

We have known leaders whose people felt they had empathy, but for whom they felt little trust. There are several possible causes for this, but we believe the most common is that their followers felt that the leader lacked consistency (for more on this, see Chapter 9). They perceived that the leader said one thing to them and then did the opposite, or said something different to someone else, or even that they constantly changed their mind.

Often, this is because the leader lacked confidence in themselves. According to research, consistency is so important in human relationships that we prefer someone to be consistently bad than someone who is unpredictable. At least we can build coping mechanisms for the consistent shortfalls of leaders.[12]

We know one law leader who is highly respected and whose people regard him with a strong sense of fondness, commitment, and trust. However, they ruefully recite instances in the past where he showed very little personal empathy, such as forgetting to ask after a close associate's health after they had just recovered from a long illness. Over time, this leader has learned to display concern for his people even when this is not top of mind. Aware of his shortcomings, he surrounds himself with associates who are high in empathy and can remind him to say the right things. He is honest, communicates frequently, keeps confidences, stands by his decisions, assumes the best of people, asks others' opinions and listens respectfully, readily accepts feedback, and admits his own mistakes. If he still has trouble feeling empathy, no one would know it.

TOP TIP

If you don't naturally feel empathy, fake it. Often, this leads to the real feeling developing!

Clear about needs and boundaries

One thing the above leader displays is a strong sense of relational and professional boundaries. He is clear about his own relational needs and expectations and those of the firm. A small example of this is that he is well organized and generous with his time, but ends meetings promptly. He does what he says he will and holds others accountable for doing the same.

With good leaders, people should know where they stand and not have to guess if the leader is pleased or displeased. Feedback should be clear, timely, and forward-looking. If there is a problem with the relationship or quality of work, there should be a discussion to explore reasons and underlying issues and agreements made about different actions going forward. A transformational leader will set or agree expectations and milestones, with regular follow-up discussions to chart progress, recalibrate, and try out different solutions.

Willing to learn and rely on others

As well as coaching others, a really transformational leader will look to grow and develop themselves. They will seek feedback and work hard to generate enough trust that people give it. They will also surround themselves with people with different views and backgrounds and expect them to challenge their views. They will facilitate genuinely generative dialogue to stimulate new ideas and innovation, and give themselves and their people time to think them through.

A transformational leader will aim to create a culture in which it is safe to try new things and fail within clearly set constraints. Does this person sound like an impossible paragon? In many ways, probably. Remember, humans are not genetically geared to be led by any one person, any more than we are geared to live in the complex, fast-changing, fractured global society that we have. Perhaps one of the most important characteristics of a good leader is that they understand this, don't try to project infallibility, and rely appropriately on those around them.

Optimistic and resilient

This inter-reliance is also key to one of the most crucial of all leadership attributes: a sense of reasonable optimism and resilience.[13] Since states of mind are contagious, the leader's optimism is essential to maintaining peoples' willingness to keep putting effort into new and better ways of meeting today's challenges. While Pollyanna-type positivity creates discomfort and skepticism and shuts down honest dialogue, a consistent sense of possibility, enthusiasm, and affirmation – especially about people – is important for an organization's success and sustainability.[14]

The key to optimism and resilience? You guessed it: surround yourself with people you trust and who meet your most important needs. Every important interaction, and often even seemingly trivial ones, affects the workings of our neurobiology and even our genetics. We display different traits with different people because, to some extent, we *are* different when we are with them. Our genes express themselves differently, our personalities change, we take on a new persona.[15]

A brain primed with dopamine and oxytocin as the result of praise and demonstrations that the person is valued will work more effectively, engender better emotional and physical health, and drive positive behaviors.[16] In this context, a person's genetic profile that normally drove, for example, pessimism and strong risk aversion might be modified to allow more upbeat comments and the consideration of new approaches. Ironically, by the way, often the last person in an organization to be overtly praised is the managing partner or leader. We find that frequently when we ask groups who they praised recently. The most hands go up for praising reports, fewer are raised in relation to colleagues, and very few people raise their hands when it comes to their leaders. Those who do raise their hands seem hesitant and sometimes sheepish.

"Praise?" exclaimed one managing partner in a break from a session we were facilitating for law leaders. "The barista downstairs gets more praise than any of us. We just get the blame!" His companions nodded appreciatively.

This is a pity, since the dopamine effect of praise is to make the brain work faster, more clearly, and more creatively – just what you want a leader's brain to do! Therefore, it seems to us that a leader should role-model asking for, and at the very least graciously receiving, praise (see Chapter 10 for more on the how-to of good praise).

Are good leaders born or taught?

Recent research suggests that the desire to be a leader is about 40 percent genetic. Though this is slightly truer of men than women (leadership has a 44 percent genetic factor for men and 37 percent for women), overall the drive for leadership seems to be highly heritable. At first, it was thought that this might just be children trying to be like their parents, but a number of recent intergenerational and twin studies have disproved this notion.[17] This does not necessarily show that good leadership is genetic; although all of the traits, and some of the skills, associated with good leadership have a strong genetic component.[18] The traits of effective leadership such as optimism, decisiveness, breadth of vision, and so forth all have a genetic base.

The genetic predisposition to lead seems simply to govern the desire to take that role, perhaps galvanized by opportunities or a strong need within the tribe. Having the will or need to be the final decision-maker will perhaps cause people to step up to or seek out the position. But unless that is paired with the right inherited characteristics and learned skills, particularly those required by the situation and organization or team, the leadership will be flawed and can even be detrimental to the firm.

Leadership in a law environment

A good leader is a good leader no matter what the organization. However, law leaders face particular environments and challenges. Much is made of the fact that, particularly in most legal partnerships, the organizational structure is fairly flat, and in many law firms crucial decisions must have a large degree of consensus. This certainly can inhibit decisions that need to be made quickly in a crisis or in periods of rapid change. However, any really good leadership requires the ability to get buy-in from people in order for strategic initiatives to be implemented and for lasting change to occur. Organizations governed by executive fiat tend to be disempowered and static.

Leadership has historically been under-appreciated in law firms. First of all, most law leaders did not rise to the position solely on the basis of their ability to galvanize and develop others; in almost all cases, they had first to be successful in the craft and business of law. In some cases, this produces an environment in which the leaders are those who were successful lawyers, but are not necessarily good managers.

People tend to revert to the success strategy that got them where they are. For a lawyer, this might be great attention to detail and an innate pessimism as to the motivations of others, coupled with a focus on the mistakes in what people are saying or doing. However, these characteristics and skills are not what an inspiring leader needs.[19] Any negativity or narrow focus of today's leaders and managers will impact not only the people and culture of today but, through a lack of inspiring role models, the leadership of the future.

Second, in many law firms, especially mid-size ones, there is still a deep distrust of management itself. There is sometimes pressure for all partners (even, in some cases, the managing partner) to stay "on the tools" and bring in income, no matter what their management responsibilities are. Managers are constantly required to justify their very position in addition to how well they do in it. "For all the respect I get, my job might just as well be shoveling manure around here", one rather disenchanted and fatigued head of a large global practice group once said to us.

One of the problems is that leadership is not seen as a career in professional service firms. Many managing partners and CEOs in law firms also feel that the top positions are more an end to their career than a rung on a ladder. "No one outside of law really believes law firms need managing", one told us. "They somehow seem to think that, unlike employees elsewhere, lawyers just get on with it themselves. So I don't think I can find a position in another type of organization. Plus, there are very few law firms looking for top leaders at a specific time, and when they do, they prefer to promote internal people who are known and know the culture." This can be a disincentive for relatively young lawyers, who may be eager to try out new ways of doing things, to seek leadership positions.

Conclusion

Great law leaders realize they cannot lead in isolation. They surround themselves with good people who support them and each other and bring different ideas and backgrounds. They have a transformational, or coaching, style and look to keep growing themselves as well as actively seeking new ideas and innovation for their firm. Their unified and dynamic leadership group provides a center that does hold and enables a firm to face the exciting and sometimes daunting challenges of our time.

References

1. Pennisi, E., "Our Egalitarian Eden", *Science*, 344:6186, pp. 824–825, 2014.

2. Turnbull, C., *The Forest People*, London, 1993.

3. Grinde, B., *Darwinian Happiness*, Chapter 9, Darwin Press, Princeton, NJ, 2002.

4. Bass, B., and Steidimeier, P., "Ethics, character, and authentic transformational leadership behavior", *The Leadership Quarterly*, 10:2, pp.181–217, 1999.

5. Eagly, A., "Women as leaders", Harvard Business School: Gender at Work research symposium, 2013.

6. Bass, B., and Riggio, R., *Transformational Leadership*, Psychology Press, Washington DC, 2006.

7. Barret-Lennard, G., *The Relationship Paradigm*, Palgrave Macmillan, New York, 2013.

8. Sutton, R., "The Boss as Human Shield," *Harvard Business Review*, September 2010.

9. Mier, R., and Giloth, R., "Cooperative Leadership", Social justice and local development policy, 1993.

10. Murray, R., and Fortinberry, A., "Rethinking Leadership Training," *Effective Executive*, 16:3, pp.40–46, 2013.

11. Goleman, D., and Boyatsis, R., "Social Intelligence and the Biology of Leadership," *Harvard Business Review*, September 1, 2008

12. Bews, N., and Rossouw, G., "A role for Business Ethics in Facilitating Trustworthiness", *Journal of Business Ethics*, 39:4, pp.377–390, 2002.

13. Avolio, B. et al, "Unlocking the mask: a look at the process by which authentic leaders impact follower attitudes and behaviors", *The Leadership Quarterly*, 15:6, pp. 801–823, 2004.

14. D'Intino, R. et al, "Self-Leadership: A Process for Entrepreneurial Success", *Journal of Leadership and Organizational Studies*, 13:4, pp.105–120, 2007.

15. Goleman, D., *Social Intelligence*, Bantam, New York, 2007.

16. Robinson, J., "In praise of praising your employees", *Gallup Business Journal*, 9 November 2006.

17. Chaturvedi, S. et al, "The heritability of emergent leadership: Age and gender as moderating factors," *The Leadership Quarterly*, 23:2, pp.219–232, 2012.

18. Dawes, C. et al, "Born to lead? A twin design and genetic association study of leadership role occupancy," *The Leadership Quarterly*, 24:1, pp.45–60, 2013.

19. Boyatzis, R., "Neuroscience and leadership: The promise of insights", *Ivey Business Journal* 75:1, pp.1–3, 2011.

Chapter 4:
The science of decision making

In this chapter we will look at:

- How humans really make decisions; and
- What are the best ways of doing so.

There has been a ton of research of late on the science of decision making. How do we decide? More importantly, what is the best way to make a decision? Is it by relying on our gut? Is it by group consensus? Is it by weighing the pros and cons? Are decisions based on reason and facts, or genes and brain chemistry? What part does experience play?

Recently, there has been a lot of argument as to whether humans have free will or not, whether there is any such thing as conscious decision making.[1] Are we locked into a combination of both biological determinism (where decisions are based on our genetics and our neurophysiology) and psychic determinism (where decisions are determined by patterns of thought based on prior – usually childhood – experiences)? Human decisions are, in fact, driven by a number of factors, as we will explore in this chapter.

The science of decision making or how do we do it?
Almost everything that is taught in business schools about decision making is based on research that is very old and from a time before we knew what actually happened in the brain and the rest of the human system when we go about making a decision. The first and most important thing to bear in mind is that almost all, maybe all, decisions are non-rational:

- They are either hardwired into our genetics; or
- Based on habitual patterns of behavior; or

- Based on assumptions and beliefs that we have built up due to experience; or

- Emotional reactions to a particular set of circumstances; or

- Dictated by the fact that we either have, or don't have, a mood disorder of some sort (as some 15–20 percent of us have at one time or another).

(A surprising number of our choices, and as some researchers have suggested, maybe all of them, are influenced by the kinds of bacteria that we have in our gut! However, this aspect is somewhat too complicated and individual-specific for us right now.)

Let's have a look at the evidence.

Our genes

All of our decisions are determined, to a greater or lesser extent, by our genes. For example, research has shown that people are predisposed by their genome (our DNA) to vote for certain kinds of political parties, to buy branded or unbranded goods, or to take out certain kinds of pension plans.[2] Our ethical and moral decisions are largely genetic in origin.[3] Even the decision to give to charity, and what charity to give to, is to a large degree determined by our genes.[4]

An obvious example of genetic predisposition is the way that individuals differ in their ability to tolerate risk. Risk tolerance is genetic; we can't "decide" to be more or less risk averse. Yet many of our decisions – from the kind of risk program we will adopt in our firm to pricing and strategy – are based on our risk tolerance or aversion.

Most of these genes, including those linked to behavior and, we believe, those associated with risk, are what we call "soft" genes. Soft genes can be influenced by experience and environment, unlike "hard" genes which dictate such things as the color of your eyes or your height, which are not environmentally influenced.

Daniel Goleman, the author of *Emotional Intelligence* and the far better but less well known book *Social Intelligence*, went so far as to say (in the latter book) that every interaction between people altered the way that their genes operated – that we, for the time of the interaction, co-create each other. He was referring to soft, not hard, genes.

What this means in practice is that when someone says they "changed their mind" about a decision after talking to someone, or having a certain experience, they are not making a comment about their cognition – their conscious thought process – but rather about the way that certain genes have altered in their expression. Your conscious mind is only making excuses for a genetically driven change.

The interesting thing is that genetically based decisions are very largely influenced by the context in which you make the decision.[5] You are liable to make a different decision if you are sitting comfortably than if you are not. A potential client will more likely hire your services, for example, if they are made to feel "at home" and comfortable. It is in this sense that you have "control" over your decisions: you can control the context in which they are made. If the context makes you feel safe, you are more likely to make a more courageous or innovative decision. If you're uncomfortable, harried, stressed, then you will more likely go for a safe, more conservative and risk-averse option.

TOP TIP

> **You cannot consciously change your genetic expression, but you can change the context in which decisions are made, and thus influence some of your own decisions and those of others.**

Our habitual responses

If you do the same thing a number of times, it becomes habitual – like many of the actions involved in driving a car to work. Each one of these actions is a decision by an unconscious part of the brain. We don't think about it, we just do it.

These habitual decisions are lodged in a part of the brain's limbic system called the basal ganglia. We need this automatic system to keep us safe. To take time making a decision when there is the danger of collision with another car or when confronted by a cheetah would be fatal.

Yet many of the so-called "higher level executive decisions" we make – to hire a particular person, or to choose a particular law firm, or to merge with another outfit – can also be driven by habitual responses and are no more conscious than putting your foot on the brake at a red light. The decision may look different from pumping the brake, and it is certainly more complex, but the impulse which drives the decision is similar to many other less complex decisions that you have taken in the past, and which have contributed to your safety.[6]

Often, these are the decisions we say are "just intuitively right". And, for you, they might well be.

TOP TIP

Ask yourself: Is this decision remotely similar to ones that are habitual? If that's the case, what would be my habitual response? You have the choice of changing the actions that lead to that habit and forming a new one.

Our assumptions and beliefs

We make decisions which are attuned to our assumptions and our beliefs. These have been built up over time as a result of our experiences – mostly childhood ones. They are the ways we interpret and make sense of the world. Every situation that we come across is assessed by what we call the "perceptual filter" which is made up of these assumptions and beliefs and which is in the part of the brain just behind the ears called the orbitofrontal cortex.

Once a belief or an assumption is lodged there it is very difficult to budge. Facts won't do it; reasoning won't touch it. If deeply embedded, it becomes part of your personality; it forms the basis of what is often called, in relation to diversity, "unconscious bias" (we all have a myriad of unconscious biases). We rarely challenge our assumptions and, anyway, most of them (about 60 percent) are totally unconscious so we couldn't even if we wanted to, at least until we become aware of them.

Once we are aware of our unconscious assumptions, we can then adopt behaviors which, hopefully, will lead to favorable outcomes. These outcomes lead to a change in the bias (i.e. we adopt another one). Because our assumptions form part of our sense of self, we find it difficult to even listen to people who challenge them. Being confronted by different views can in extreme cases prompt the well-known "amygdala hijack", in which the brain's safety circuit takes over the whole functioning of the brain and prevents new information from entering. This is one of the reasons why we don't hear up to 60 percent of what people say. In fact, our brains are constantly engaged in this selective listening, filtering out those things that we find awkward or not in line with our preconceptions.

According to most researchers, it is almost impossible for a human to reach a decision that is contrary to either a core belief or a hidden assumption. This is seen most clearly in what is called "evidentiary bias" in decision making: the bias to act according to what we already believe or assume, and to disregard or reinterpret contradictory evidence.

One of the core values that a large firm we know cites with pride is making "evidence-based decisions". Humans like to think that we weigh any decision carefully, rather than rushing headlong to a conclusion. How many times have you been advised to "weigh all the pros and cons" before coming to a decision? How many times have you advised people to do this? In fact, as recent scientific research has shown us, this exercise is quite useless in terms of actually making an "unbiased" decision.

The brain looks through the evidence before us searching for "facts" that will confirm our assumptions and stops seriously looking when we find them. We have "made up our mind" by confirming our own beliefs or assumptions – even if we continue the process of "weighing the pros and cons".

This is even true in medicine where the health outcomes, and even lives, of millions of people may be at stake. Researchers in this field, too, are biased towards evidence that confirms what they already believe, and tend to ignore that which does not fit into their preexisting assumptions.[7]

TOP TIP

Your hidden assumptions will be reflected in your past choices. Examine all of the decisions you have made over the last couple of years and work out what your hidden assumptions are.

Our emotions

It has long been recognized that our decisions are not based on reason but emotion. The strongest of these is fear, particularly fear of loss.[8] A few years ago, researchers discovered what is now called behavioral economics. They found that the "rational economic man (or woman)" does not exist and that we are far more swayed by our emotions in economic decision making than by the facts presented to us. They discovered that we are motivated by fear of loss far more than we are by promise of gain. Because we are afraid that we will incur loss, we opt for the immediate reward rather than a greater one later (even a day later).

More recently, researchers have found that these same drivers exist in rhesus monkeys and, given that they are a long way from us in evolutionary branching, these tendencies must have been embedded in our genes and those our ancestors for the last 35 million years.[9]

Fear dominates all our decisions, not just our economic ones. This is true even of those whose genetics predispose them to take greater risks; it just means that the loss that's feared is different.

Often, the loss that poses the greatest threat is the loss of supportive relationships. We fear exclusion; in fact, we fear it more than death and we will often do quite irrational things to try to overcome it.[10] Many of our decisions, good and bad, are based on this fear.

In evolutionary terms, it makes sense to base our actions and our decisions on a dread of being excluded from our tribe. In hunter-gatherer times, separation from the band meant almost certain death, so over the millions of years of our existence before the advent of farming, the need to remain part of a supportive group became embedded in our genes. It became our primary driving force.

The most striking example of this is the decision made by radical Islamic suicide bombers to carry out their acts of carnage. It is commonly thought – and repeated by many commentators – that these people do what they do because they believe in the cause of Islam, or that they will go to heaven and be surrounded by virgins. The problem, these experts say, is that the decision to suicide is based on a perverted theology, or their misreading of the Koran, or their misinterpretation of the sayings of the prophet.

The evidence, from studies of those whose explosives failed to go off, shows that the motivation is quite different. They may believe passionately in Islam and in the particular strain of the religion. They may even believe that they will have the virgins, but these do not motivate the killing. Religion is a rationalization of another, deeper motive. By and large these people have not previously shown any suicidal tendencies and, despite coming from generally dysfunctional homes, the majority are not depressed or suffering from some other psychiatric disorder.

The motive, the driver, is that they feel that they will be a more valued member of the group they have chosen to identify with if they volunteer to carry out the act, and that they may be excluded if they do not carry it out. Their death – and the deaths of the people they murder – are perpetrated to solidify a relationship that they feel is, or has been, supportive to them.[11] The mass suicide in Jonestown in 1978 when over 900 members of a religious sect led by Jim Jones drank cyanide and died is another case in point.

Your decision to move your firm in a particular direction, and your followers' decisions to agree with your conclusion, will at least in part be based on your and their need to avoid the loss of a supportive relationship. Maybe not consciously; the real reasons for any decision are rarely conscious, but hidden deep in that which makes us human. Your decision is, neurogenetically speaking, fundamentally the same as a suicide bomber's. Your brain is basically asking: "Whom do I need to please?"

Often, fraud and other criminal acts are committed to strengthen relationships, to show that the particular fraudster is part of the same tribe as the others, and to thus avoid being excluded. This is true, for example, of people who hide the loss of large sums of money in order to be seen as successful, and thus accepted, by a firm. There have been a number of such cases in major law firms over the last few years.

However, fear of exclusion also has its good side. It helps to keep otherwise too-powerful people in check, and it often makes it difficult for overly disruptive people to do too much harm. The main point here is that people's fear of exclusion – loss of relational support – is a powerful, unconscious, motivator of decisions good or bad.

Overwhelmingly, then, our decisions are based on factors beyond our conscious, our rational, control rather than on facts or reason. These are only called upon ex-post facto to justify a decision that the unconscious brain has already arrived at.

Ask yourself who you are trying to please or avoid offending by making one decision rather than another.

The effect of mood disorders

Science is not sure what causes major depression, general anxiety disorder, bipolar disorder (manic depression), and the like. What we do know is that they have a profound effect on the decisions we make, and indeed impair the decision-making process as a whole.[12] Mood disorders, especially depression or anxiety, cause all cognitive processes to slow down and, as we will show below, this makes for worse decision outcomes. These and other disorders also make us less sure about our decisions and, more importantly here, direct decision making towards outcomes that may well be self-destructive or harmful to others. This is an unconscious process and the affected person will have no idea that this is what they are doing.

How to make the best decisions

All is not lost! There are ways of making effective decisions – just, perhaps, not ways that we were taught, or we're used to. We don't want to rehash all of the material in thousands of books and articles in the popular press or learned journals on decision making. Most of them were written by management consultants, not scientists. However there are two ways of arriving at a good decision that we, as scientists, would recommend. They are:

- Trust your gut; and
- Decide by group consensus.

Both of these approaches will be about 60 percent more accurate than any other decision-making protocol. This is because neither allows a couple of the problems listed above to have undue sway.

Trust your gut

In his marvelous book *Blink*, Malcolm Gladwell speaks of the power of gut decisions, how we are wired to make them, and of their accuracy. Overwhelmingly, the research that has been carried out since then has shown that the essential message of the book is correct. As the great Chinese strategist Sun Tsu wrote 2,500 years ago in his text *The Art of War*, human beings are made for what he called "situation/react" or immediate response to any state of affairs.[13] What both Gladswell and Sun Tsu were getting at is that, in decision-making terms, humans are wired for action, not deliberation.

Gladswell speaks of traders on the floor of the New York Stock Exchange having to make lightning-fast choices, and the remarkable number of times in which they get it right. In the laboratory or class-room, we can use deliberative skills and decision trees to help us work our way through masses of data and options. In the real world, as he says, that is all thrown aside. We can never know or understand all the data, and our brains are not, in any case, built for complexity. Our neurogenetic system is geared to instantaneously size up a situation and react. One of the reasons for that is that we will never know whether a decision is right or wrong, except in hindsight. This is true no matter how many hours you pore over the decision tree or the data.

In the time of our remote ancestors on the savannah of East Africa, situations were much less complex than they are today. They had to avoid dangers that could appear very suddenly and doing so required very, very, fast decision and reaction speeds. The fastest survived. Over time, speed of decision making became what is known as "adaptive", and so encoded in our DNA and hard wired in our neural circuitry.

Instantaneously, the brain gets to the crux of any situation and decides on a suitable action. In reality, no individual decision takes more than a couple of seconds. On the savannah, that's the time you had before the cheetah saw you and made her run. In fact, the part of the brain which is responsible for coordinating snap decisions – the anterior cingulate cortex (ACC) – can do its job in one-twentieth of a second. In that time, it directs our attention and coordinates our thoughts, emotions, and the body's response to our feelings.

It can work that quickly because of what are called spindle cells. These wonderful cells are much larger than other cells in the cortex and they are able to make many, many more connections than other neurons. The great apes (chimpanzees, gorillas, bonobos, orangutans, and us) are the only animals that have spindle cells, and humans have thousands more than any of the others. This is probably because other animals – including the apes – have far more means of escape and defense than we do. Our decision speed is our only reliable defense mechanism.

The spindles carry the sensory information (the look of threat on the face of the aggressor, the twitch on the side of the mouth indicating a lie, the movement of a stock price) to the ACC and beyond and the appropriate decision is made. All of this without the conscious mind being involved.[14]

Very recent research has shown that many of these decisions may well not be made by the cerebral cortex at all, but by other neural circuits or "brains" in other parts of the body – the heart,[15] the gut,[16] the skin[17] – which then send the decision to the cortex for action. These, the researchers say, act at the same kind of speed as the cortex. However you look at it, decision speed is indeed in our DNA.

Many studies have shown that the initial gut decision can be over-ridden by reflection. But these same studies show that, if we do ignore our gut, our eventual choice will likely be much worse. Our perceptual filter gets in the way, our evidential bias rules supreme. Given time, we tend to make the same choice everyone else is making – lemmings heading to the cliff face. You see this in strategy decisions some law firms have made; the tendency has been to decide by fad.

Learn to trust your gut.

Group decision making

Group judgments are more accurate than individual ones up to 90 percent of the time.[18] Looking again at our hunter-gatherer ancestors, one of the interesting things about their decision making was the way in which they tackled large decisions. Bob lived with hunter-gatherers for about a year and observed the way in which they went about it. A really important decision – such as to move to a new hunting ground, to trade with another band who shared a different totem, or to swap hunting for fishing – was taken by consensus by everyone over the age of six. They would take as long as needed for everyone to agree. This is the idea behind jury trials, of course. Similar decision making has been witnessed by other researchers studying modern hunter-gatherers in Africa, South America, and (before 1930) in Australia.[19]

Almost all of the research has shown that group decisions are, on the whole, superior to those made by an individual. There are some kinks, however, which can tend to reduce the effectiveness of the group. The decision-making group should have a number of essential characteristics (much like the strategy group that we discuss in Chapter 7). It must be diverse in background, gender, and outlook; otherwise, it will fall prey to group think, no matter how many walls they write on and no matter how different the ideas they come up with look to those involved. Also, the group should contain at least one subject expert.

CASE STUDY

Humans are attracted to those with whom they have a lot in common, and the same thing is true of law leaders. Bob watched the managing partner at a large international firm choose a group of people who would be tasked with helping him decide on whether to move their head office into an open-plan space in a building a short distance away or remain where they were.

The group was formed of partners and the COO. The MP dominated the discussions and during all the time Bob observed the discussions there were few, if any, genuinely dissenting voices and very few questions. It was clear that they all shared the same assumptions, backgrounds, and concerns. It was group think from the beginning to the end. The "decision" to move to the new open space building was obvious from the first meeting. It was what the MP wanted.

Another firm, a mid-size Chicago-based practice, was faced with the same issue and, again, Bob was privileged to be a part of the discussion. In this case, the MP made the choice to take a back seat in the decision process. The members of the group tasked with making the choice were chosen at random and they included two partners (one male and one female), two senior associates (both female), a junior lawyer (male), the HR head (female), and the receptionist (male).

In this group there was fierce debate, and a lot of laughter. During the 10 working days that they had to come up with their answer, they developed camaraderie. Mutual support was evident and, most important of all, they listened to each other without criticism and asked questions which showed that they were genuinely interested. They visited the proposed new building and several others which had the same kind of open space to see how they actually worked and talked to people who worked there. All of which they enjoyed. They also co-opted an expert not involved with the proposed open space to sit in with them. In the end, they decided that they were better off where they were.

Interestingly, the decision by the larger firm has been proven to be wrong – most people, especially the partners, didn't like the space – and the "open space" has become much like the space they left with the "meeting spaces" and "quiet spaces" becoming de facto offices for the senior partners, much to the annoyance of the rest who have no place to make confidential client telephone calls. The decision by the more diverse group was the better one, for that firm at that time.

One of the interesting things about group decision making, both in humans and in animals, is that there seems to be a transfer of information, without formal signaling or words, between members of the group. Welcome to the weird and wonderful world of mirror cells (which enable us to feel what others feel) and other brain functions. We know that humans, just by being together, are smarter. For example, students sitting exams in a room with other people – even if those others are not sitting the same exams – do better than when they are sitting them in a room by themselves. Brains work faster together, and on average, much more accurately.

There is such a thing as a kind of group mind-meld – not the Vulcan trick from Star Wars – which was recently proven in a study showing direct human brain-to-brain communication was possible.[20]

Animal studies have shown that this seems to be true, especially if one member of the decision-making group has deep knowledge of that which the decision is about.[21] In fact, having an expert as part of the decision team has another distinct advantage – their brains work differently during the decision process and thus give an added dimension to the way the problem at hand is considered. An expert with a deep knowledge of their subject, will use a "working forward" approach. That is, their brain will take the knowledge that they have and the information given to work forward to a solution.

In contrast, neophytes employ a "working back" from the perceived outcome or goal to arrive at a decision. A deep knowledge expert – like a London cab driver, or a property lawyer, or a medical specialist, or as in the case study above, an expert in open space working – will have a larger hippocampal region where their knowledge is stored and different pathways from there to the brain areas (basal ganglia, striatum, cordate nucleus, ventral prefrontal cortex) where decision making takes place.

This depth of knowledge can also bias any decision, which is why a panel of experts can also fall prey to group think. An expert in a branch of law is liable to see any problem from the perspective of the area of their own expertise. They might find it difficult to be "commercial" for example, or "flexible". So, while it is often imperative that a subject expert be on the decision-making panel, it is dangerous to leave the decision totally in the expert's hands.

Unfortunately, in our experience, the way most law leaders and other managers (including politicians) use decision groups is unfortunate. What tends to happen is that the MP, or other leader, sets up a decision group and then cherry-picks the information or answers they receive. The bits, or the decisions they pick are most likely to be those that are in line with their own ideas. This, of course, destroys the whole benefit of having the group in the first place.

Conclusion

The ways we go about making decisions – as individuals and in groups – are often less than optimal. Following the "10 virtuous actions of decision making" can help you overcome assumptions, bias, and habitual responses, to make sounder decisions. The 10 virtuous actions are:

1. Go over all your last year's decisions and find out what your hidden assumptions are;

2. Make a list of all your assumptions and beliefs about a decision and work out how to test them;

3. Ask yourself: "What would my habitual response to this situation be?";

4. Observe yourself when you're looking at evidence: When does your evidentiary bias kick in?;

5. Starting with unimportant decisions, learn to trust your gut;

6. For major decisions, form a diverse group to be the decision makers;

7. Make sure that there is at least one subject matter expert on the panel;

8. Get out of the way and let them get on with it;

9. Have the courage to accept their decision; and

10. Remember that you will only know whether a decision is the right one in retrospect.

References

1. See Harris, S., *Free Will*, Free Press, New York, 2012.

2. Cesarini, D. et al, "Genetic Variation in Financial Decision-Making." *The Journal of Finance*, 65: 1725–1754, 2010.

3. Marsh, A. et al, "Serotonin Transporter Genotype (5-HTTLPR) Predicts Utilitarian Moral Judgments" PLOS-One, pub, 2011.

4. Cesarini, D. et al, "Genetic Variation in Preferences for Giving and Risk Taking" MIT Open, 2009; available at http://dspace.mit.edu/handle/1721.1/57904.

5. Reiss, D. and Leve, L., "Genetic expression outside the skin: Clues to mechanisms of Genotype × Environment interaction" *Development and Psychopathology* 19:4, pp 1005–1027, 2007.

6. Johnson, J. and Basenmeyer, J., "Rule-based Decision Field Theory" in Tilmann Betch ed, *The Routines of Decision Making*, Psychology Press, Washington DC, 2014.

7. Maurice, C. et al, "Reporting data: managing sampling and analytical uncertainty" *Future Medicine*, February 2014 pp 88–101, 2014.

8. Pessoa, L., "Quantitative prediction of perceptual decisions during near-threshold fear detection" *PNAS*, 102:15 pp 5612–5617, 2005.

9. Santos, L. et al, "The Evolutionary roots of human decision making" *Annual Review of Psychology*, 2015.

10. Beaumeister, R. et al, "Social Exclusion Causes People to Spend and Consume Strategically in the Service of Affiliation" *Journal of Consumer Research*, 37: 5 pages 902–919, 2011.

11. Kruglanski, A. et al, "Fully Committed: Suicide Bombers' Motivation and the Quest for Personal Significance", *Political Psychology*, 30:3 pages 331–357, 2009. Haque, O. et al, "Why Are Young Westerners Drawn to Terrorist Organizations Like ISIS?" *Psychiatric Times*, 10 September 2015.

12. Murphy, F.C. et al, "Decision-making in mania and depression" *Psychological Medicine* 31:4, pp 679–693, 2001.

13. Sun Tsu, *The Art of War*, Filiguarian edition, 2007.

14. Courtney, S., "Information Storage and Executive Control May Not Be So Separate after All" *Neuron*, 87:4, pp 861–863, 2015.

15. McCratney, R., "Heart-Brain Neurodynamics: The Making of Emotions" *Neuropsychotherapist*, Special issue 2015, pp 76–110, 2015.

16. Mayer, E., "Gut feelings: the emerging biology of gut-brain interactions" *Nature Reviews Neuroscience* 12, pp 453–466, 2011.

17. Pruszynski, J.A. and Johansson, R.S., "Edge-orientation processing in first-order tactile neurons" *Nature Neuroscience*, 17, pp 1404–1409, 2014.

18. Mannes, A.E., "Are we wise about the wisdom of crowds? The use of group judgments in belief revision" *Management Science* 55, pp 1267–1279, 2009.

19. See e.g. Turnbull, C., *The Forest People*, Pimlico, London, 1993.

20. Rao, R. and Stocco, A., "When to brains connect" *Scientific American Mind* 25, pp 36–39.

21. Couzin, I. et al, "Effective leadership and decision-making in animal groups on the move" *Nature* 433, pp 513–516, 2005. Conradt, L., "Group decision making in animals" *Nature* 421, pp 155–158, 2003.

Chapter 5:
Creating the right culture for your organization

In this chapter we:

- Consider the issue of culture and culture change; and
- Offer some practical "how-tos" for creating a viable and productive culture that will enable law firms to flourish in the "new normal".

"I want to get my partners to adopt a more entrepreneurial, cooperative culture", the CEO of a mid-sized American law firm told us recently. He wanted our team to come up with instant answers to the question of how he should go about doing this. There had already been a couple of failed attempts to change the culture of the firm. We believed the reason for the failures was that the ideas behind the change programs were not based on what science now knows to be the real drivers of human behavior and the willingness of people to change.

It is a common misconception that an organizational culture can be summed up by a series of vague quasi-value terms such as "integrity", "entrepreneurial", "excellence", or "respect". These often tend to be managerial wish lists rather than any real description of what people actually believe or the way they actually behave.

Most firms, even medium-sized ones, will probably have a number of sub-cultures, some of which may even be mutually antagonistic. This was certainly true of the one we were working with. This mutual antagonism, and the accompanying suspicion, is one of the reasons why over 70 percent of culture change programs fail.[1]

As we have seen, the reason humans adopt or create any particular culture is to surround themselves with a nexus of people who will support them. We are genetically geared to look for, and to rely on, that support.[2] Therefore, an organization's culture is reflected in the way that people behave towards each other on a day-to-day basis: how they greet each other, how they socialize, how they use praise, and in many other small everyday rituals. It is rare that law leaders look at culture in this way.

In this chapter, we examine the issue of culture and culture change through the lens of the latest findings from a number of fields – neurogenetics, anthropology, and evolutionary psychology – along with our consulting perspective. We will also offer some practical "how-tos" for any managing partner wanting to create a culture that will enable their firm to flourish in this fast-changing and puzzling "new normal".

The main thing that we want to emphasize throughout this chapter is that any culture is a complex interaction between people, involving shared values, rituals, language, assumptions, and beliefs, and all of these elements are reflected in behaviors. Indeed, it can be said that the behavioral norms of a culture are often what drive the creation of the other aspects of it.[3]

Once established, cultures, like individuals, are often very resistant to change. This resistance comes largely from ingrained habit and also from threat. If a group feels under threat or pressure it will emphasize the differences between it and any other group it feels threatened by. Often, this is the firm's management. Openness to change comes from a sense of safety and the exposure of the group to, and development of commonalities with, other cultures.[4]

Getting the right culture

The task of management, therefore, is to create the conditions under which the majority of the firm's employees and partners are willing and able to change. The human brain and genome (our individual and collective DNA) are largely social tools. They have evolved to allow us to get on with others of our species. There are a number of actions that management can take which will work with this evolution. Unfortunately, the majority of the time the way that leadership tries to direct culture change – as with the managing partner of the law firm we mentioned at the start of this chapter – goes against both human evolution and human genetics.

To be in tune with human genetics and human neurobiology there are a number of actions that management can take, and in doing so ensure that they get the right culture for the business to prosper. These are:

- Bring people into the decision-making process around the new culture;
- Adopt a transformational leadership style;

- Build the new culture around a purpose or a vision which the people see as important;
- Concentrate on behaviors, not on attitudes or states of mind;
- Create a climate of safety, making it okay to experiment with new ways of behaving – humans only change when they feel safe; and
- Allow the culture to grow organically.

Doing these things will go a long way to creating the kind of aligned culture which can move an organization to change and towards creating the conditions for a strategy to succeed.

Get people involved in decision making

Before you even embark on the exercise of behavioral change, you need to explain the "why" of the change; for example, why the individuals, and by extension the firm, need to be more entrepreneurial, more cooperative. More importantly, you need to listen to their ideas and, perhaps, their objections. You should concentrate on working with them, not against them. In that way, they will feel an integral part of the process, which is essential.

By bringing the partners and other employees of the firm into the decision-making process in this way, you are making decisions in the way that hunter-gatherer bands come to decisions.[5] You are breaking down hierarchy and working with human genetics. No known hunter-gatherer band has, in normal times, a definitive hierarchy or leadership, and this universality of equality in decision making can only be explained by genetics.[6]

Adopt a transformational leadership style

A leadership style which goes with the grain of human nature is far more likely to be effective than one which does not, and the style which is most attuned to the way in which our neurogenetics actually work is the one often called transformational leadership (as described in the previous chapter).[7]

In terms of change management, this is a style of leadership where the leader identifies the needed change, creates a vision or a purpose, and guides the change through giving inspiration, showing influence, and demonstrating support for individuals. The leader executes the change in tandem with members of the group. Through these actions, they get people committed to the relationship with the leader, to the project, and to the success of the firm as a whole.

A transformational leader will also understand that the way they communicate their ideas is vitally important. People must not only be brought into the decision-making process, the communication should be face-to-face as far as possible.

In large firms like many we have worked for, this direct face-to-face communication between the leader and the workforce is not always possible. Leaders of these enterprises often rely on video presentations to get their message across. Because humans scan facial muscles and other signs for truth-telling, these videos often get the eye-roll effect and are seen as distancing the leader from the rest of the firm. It is far better for the leader to communicate the message to their direct reports and for them to pass down the communication face to face. If the culture has to be spread through an organization comprising virtual teams, then the leader should use whatever teleconference, Skype, or other means to deliver the message as closely to face-to-face as is possible.[8]

This concept of face-to-face communication is another means for creating safety. Humans are far more ready to accept an idea if it is communicated personally. We are face-to-face animals; it is by the judgment of our senses that we decide whether to trust or not.[9] As this method of communication and decision making on significant issues is preferred universally in societies everywhere, the desire for it must, again, be embedded in our genes.[10]

A transformational leader will gain far more commitment than one who adopts a more transactional or "do as I say!" style. Their people will change in order to strengthen the bond between themselves and the leader. A transformational leader makes their people feel safe, even protected, and one of the things that we know is that people only really change when they feel safe.

Build your culture around a purpose

In order for a firm to have an entrepreneurial culture (or any other kind of culture), there must be some overarching rationale for that culture in terms of the individual as well as for the firm as a whole. The firm is the primary tribe for most people. It is within this tribe that people find safety and community, and as long as they believe that this is the case, they will support efforts to preserve it.[11]

Part of this safety comes from the knowledge that the council of elders in a hunter-gatherer band – or parents in terms of a family or management in a law business – knows where they're going, that they have a purpose. In hunter-gatherer times, the purpose was simple: the survival of the band.

Every purpose that a modern family or enterprise might adopt is simply a variation on the theme of tribal survival. In these times of the "new normal", when there is little increase in the pool of money available for purchases, top-line revenue for a firm can often only be increased by gaining market share from their competitors or through innovation in the way they operate. Therefore, a modern culture change may well begin with the purpose of satisfying the customer more than other firms can.[12]

Essentially, "perfecting our client experience" is neurogenetically the same as "moving to a better hunting ground". The purpose must be communicated to the workforce – the tribal members – as an issue of survival in ways that they understand and which are meaningful to them. And, of course, in ways that show that they have input into the decision.

Focus on changing behaviors, not attitudes

Let's say that, as part of the purpose of being the best at discovering and satisfying the needs of your clients, you want to introduce a more entrepreneurial, cooperative culture. The first thing to realize is that these terms are very general and can mean many things to many people. Rather than worrying about the meaning of the words, ask yourself what actions you are looking for. What do you actually want your people to *do* differently?

Remember that you know a culture by the things that people do, not by the thoughts that go on in their heads. Since you cannot read those, you can never know people's thoughts and attitudes, only their behaviors. For example, in terms of being more entrepreneurial and cooperative, do you want them to:

- Regularly brainstorm new ideas with each other?
- Spend more time doing business development?
- Get to know their clients' business more thoroughly?
- Ask questions to perhaps discover problems that the clients did not even know they had?
- Listen more intently to what their clients are telling them before rushing in with solutions?
- Work as a team with others to fully meet clients' needs?

These and other behaviors will almost certainly come up when you put it to a focus groups of the partnership, or the employees generally, and ask them what new actions they would adopt to be more entrepreneurial and cooperative. Management teams rarely do this. Yet, in terms of how the brain works, it is far more likely that people will adhere to behaviors that they themselves have come up with.[13]

You will also get greater agreement as to what rewards are applicable for compliance and what penalties will apply for non-compliance. A good change leader knows that these are better coming from the bottom-up in an organization rather than from the top down. In terms of the rewards that the leader personally gives people, these should be in the form of praise and recognition. Monitory rewards and bonuses, no matter how eagerly sought by the partnership and others, are self-defeating since they tend to be "normalized" as part of their normal remuneration and expected going forward without extra work.[14]

Once you have arrived at an agreement about concrete behaviors under a particular value, and what sanctions would apply if people do not behave accordingly, you have begun to change the culture. There need not be many such agreed actions – perhaps only two or three under each of the firm's values – for the change to take place. These become what we call "catalyst" behaviors because they lead to the gradual development and adoption of a range of other accepted behaviors. What the group members are doing is building a tribe where adherence to the agreed norms of behavior becomes the essence of belonging. The whole human system is geared towards acceptance and belonging, and this, as we said earlier, is why we have a culture in the first place.

Of course, entrepreneurialism is not the only value that you will want to establish as the basis of the new culture. There will be a range of others which together will form the basis of the "right" culture for your business. For each of these, you will go through the same process of discovering the concrete behaviors that will indicate to you and the other members of the tribe that the value is being adhered to. If, for example, there are five values that you want to instill as part of the culture, then you may wind up with a catalyst list of about 10 behaviors – a kind of behavioral charter (see, for example, the behavioral charter in Chapter 9).

Create a sense of safety for experiment

One of the most important things that management can do to encourage a new, and more productive, culture is to make it safe for people to experiment with new behaviors and different ways of working. Some of these will turn out to be less than optimal, and some will seem strange to the business leaders. But the increased feeling of autonomy and the often extremely beneficial ideas that come forth make it well worthwhile.

The essence of safety in this context is the art of catching people doing things right rather than concentrating on what they are doing wrong. Very often, there is a lot right with an experiment that goes wrong. For example, when Motorola was looking to develop a radically new mobile phone back in the 1980s they looked at all their competitors' failed experiments and asked themselves "what were they doing right?" not "what did they do wrong?". By building on the "right" rather than getting sidetracked by the "wrong" they were able to develop the famous flip-top phone.

The same process is true in the development of a culture. Watch what people are doing, then praise and build on what they do right, rather than focusing on what they do wrong.[15] An important finding from recent research is that people learn from being praised for what they do right and not, as we used to think, from their mistakes. In fact, concentrating on what people do wrong only leads to their doing the wrong things more often.[16] When people feel safe and appreciated, they become open to change, and those changes which are acknowledged and praised will stick.[17]

Allow the culture to develop organically

The beauty of having catalyst behaviors in place is that the rest of the elements of a culture will begin to fall into place naturally as a result of adhering to them. The important thing is to allow the culture to develop organically, for when management gets impatient and tries to rush the process, it very rarely succeeds.[18] The leadership of the enterprise must take more of a back seat, as it's not exclusively their culture that is being developed; they are merely a part of it. The rest of the process comes from the bottom up.

What management *can* do is allow the space and the opportunities for the culture to develop. Allow opportunities for socializing, within and outside working hours. Give people the chance to share ideas and to develop new rituals. A ritual can be as simple as going for drinks together after work, eating lunch together, saying hello in the morning, or meeting more often face to face rather than by email.

Don't worry if, at first, some of the new culture seems to be "anti-management" – a transformational leader accepts this as natural. They will adhere to the behaviors, discuss shared beliefs and assumptions, and adopt some of the new jargon.

Conclusion

The science of human behavior shows us how to create a viable and productive culture. It means concentrating on behaviors rather than abstract concepts of what the culture ought to be like. For an enterprise's leadership, this means letting go of some of the older management styles and working with the employees as a trusting team. We have found that this works even in businesses where there has traditionally been a high level of conflict between the management and the workforce.

References

1. Micheli, P., "Why Strategies Fail to be Executed", *Management Focus*, Autumn 2011, p 25, 2011.
2. Baumeister, R.F. and Leary, M.R., "The need to belong: Desire for interpersonal attachments as a fundamental human motivation", *Psychological Bulletin*, Vol. 117 No. 3, pp 497-429, (1995)
3. Cooke, R.A. et al, "Dysfunctional culture, dysfunctional organization: Capturing the behavioral norms that form organizational culture and drive performance", *Journal of Managerial Psychology*, Vol. 21 No. 8, pp 709 – 732, 2006.
4. Jones A.L., *Cultures Merging*, Princeton University Press, 2009.
5. Turnbull, C., *The Forest People*, Touchstone Publishing, New York, 1987.
6. Pennisi, E., "Our Egalitarian Eden", *Science*, 23 May 2014, pp 824–825, 2014.
7. Bass, B. and Riggio, R., *Transformational Leadership*, Laurence Erlbaum Publishers, Mahwah, NJ, 2006.
8. Purvanova, R. and Bono, J., "Transformational leadership in context: Face-to-face and virtual teams", *The Leadership Quarterly*, Vol. 20, No. 3, pp 343–357, 2009.
9. Golden, T.D. et al, "The impact of professional isolation on teleworker job performance and turnover intentions: Does time spent teleworking, interacting face-to-face, or having access to communication-enhancing technology matter?", *Journal of Applied Psychology*, Vol. 38 No. 6, , 2008, pp. 1412–1421.
10. Cosmides, L. and Tooby, J., "Better than Rational: Evolutionary Psychology and the invisible hand", *American Economic Review*, Vol. 84 No. 2, 1994, pp. 327–340.
11. Wilcock, K.D., *Hunting and Gathering in the Corporate Tribe*, Volume 1, Algora Publishing, New York, 2004.
12. Ulrich, D. et al, "Building culture from the outside in," *Strategic HR Review*, Vol. 8 No. 6, 2009, pp. 20–27.
13. Norcross, J.C. et al, "Auld Lang Syne: Success predictors, change processes, and self-reported outcomes of New Year's resolvers and nonresolvers", *Journal of Clinical Psychology*, Vol. 58 No. 4, 2002, pp. 397–405.

14. Izyma, K. et al, "Processing of monetary and social rewards in the human striatum", *Neuron* Vol. 58, No 2, 2008, pp. 284–294.
15. Cooperrider, D.L. and Whitney D., *Appreciative Inquiry*, Berrett-Koehler Publishers, San Francisco, 2005.
16. Histed, M. et al, "Learning Substrates in the Primate Prefrontal Cortex and Striatum: Sustained Activity Related to Successful Actions", *Neuron*, Vol. 63, No. 2, 2009, pp. 244–253.
17. O'Tool, M., "The relationship between employees' perceptions of safety and organizational culture", *Journal of Safety Research*, Vol. 33 No. 2, 2002, pp. 231–243.
18. Choueke, R. and Armstrong, R., "Culture: a missing perspective on small- and medium-sized enterprise development?", *International Journal of Entrepreneurial Behavior & Research*, Vol. 6 No. 4, 2000, pp.227–238.

Chapter 6:
Getting commitment to change

In this chapter we look at:

- Why people resist change;
- The assumptions that create resistance;
- The use, and misuse, of influencers;
- How to overcome resistance in individuals and firms; and
- How to make change stick.

Many consultants and other gurus claim that people should "embrace change" as if that were something that you could do simply by trying. Their pontifications have found a special place in the hearts of some law firm leaders. "All I need to do", the managing partner of a mid-sized US law firm told us just before a presentation we gave at the Mid-Western Law Forum conference a couple of years ago, "is to get the partners to embrace change – to see that the changes I'm suggesting are good for them".

The pity of it is that humans don't work that way. They do not generally accept change because it is "good for them" – otherwise every child would eat their greens and no adult would smoke or drink to excess. I fear that this managing partner would have remained disappointed.

However, all is not lost. Humans do not like to change, but they can be *persuaded* to, and recent discoveries in human science show how this can be done. This chapter is about how to get people genuinely to commit to change and also how to make change successful. We'll be looking at the latest science in the area of change and suggesting ways to get around the knee-jerk resistance that we all have to it.

Why people resist change

Resistance to change is inbuilt; it's in our genes and in our neuro-biology. The neural pathways that any call to change goes through are the same ones that carry messages about physical and emotional pain. Change can make us ill, both mentally and physically. Any change which threatens to affect a person's life in a major way can cause the system to overproduce the kind of neurochemicals (principally cortisol) which, in excess, can cause major mental and physical illness. Those that look at the context – particularly the social context – of change, have pointed out that anything that threatens to change a person's network of relational support (family, office, friendships) causes potentially damaging stress.[1]

When you, as a law leader, ask your people to make a change that is going to affect them in ways which threaten to alter their social context, you are asking them to put their health, and possibly their life, at risk. It's not the way corporate or firm CEOs – with their eyes on the balance sheet and the profit and loss figures – normally think. As a leader, your social context may not be threatened by the changes – in fact, if your social network is largely other law leaders, others in your C-suite, or corporate CEOs or political leaders, you may not be in any serious way affected by the change. You do not see the potential damage your brilliant new ideas may cause.

Any leader contemplating any significant change must realize that the greatest fear that humans have is of exclusion, or a fundamental disruption of their social relationships. Any change which threatens that will cause problems which will render the change initiative difficult at best. The threat of unemployment is harmful largely because it means exclusion from, perhaps, our main social nexus.

Although this is true for both sexes, it is truer for men than women.[2] Again, this is genetic. Men are wired to get their greatest social connection from those that they hunt with. Women tend to bond with a greater circle of people and have the ability to build vibrant social support systems outside of the work tribe. They have a greater neural ability to expand their connections. Retirement, or the threat of being laid off, is neurogenetically harder for men than women. However, as with men, women's sense of self-worth may be tied up with their career, and they may fear that losing a job may hinder their acceptance by their wider social network.

TOP TIP

When planning for change, take people's fear of social change into account. Emphasize continuity of relationships.

The assumptions that create resistance

In times of change, both leaders and those they lead are blinded by their assumptions, most of which are wrong, but all of which are based on their genes and their experience. Unconsciously, most of us assume that others believe the same things we do, and that there's something wrong with them if they don't. We feel that our assumptions and beliefs are the "natural" and "rational" ones to have about any situation.

However, other than a belief such as that 1+1=2, there are no rational beliefs. Your assumption, for example, that "digitizing our knowledge management will benefit the firm" is not a rational belief like 1+1=2. Rather, it is built upon a foundation of your experience and your genome.

You say, "look at the facts", or "look at the savings", or "look at the increase in efficiency", and you are just looking at what you are predisposed to look at. You are not looking at what the other person is looking at, the things that matter to them: their fears, their assumptions, and their motivations.

Assumptions based on biology

What you are predisposed to look at is often governed by the non-rational parts of your biology, by your genetic inheritance. Here are some examples.

1. You are probably genetically inclined to be a leader

About 40 percent of all leaders have the same expression of a particular cluster of genes that dispose a person to either be a leader or a follower.[3] In terms of genetics, this is a high correlation. You will see the world from the perspective of that genetic predisposition. Leaders with that genetic predisposition are more likely to insist that they are right and are unlikely to listen to contrary opinions, or if they do, to admit that they have any validity.[4]

A few years ago, we were brought in to help a mid-sized firm. The managing partner was a man in his early fifties who wanted to make the business more "client responsive". "It is so obvious", he told us, "that this is the virtue that the firm needs".

We asked him what "client responsiveness" meant. "Every partner knows that", he answered in disbelief that we should ask such a silly question.

Later, we were doing a workshop for 15 of the firm's most senior partners and we asked them, anonymously, to write down what they thought it meant. Each one had a different answer from "being knowledgeable about the law" to "answering my mobile at all times".

Later, we showed the MP the answers. "They just don't get it", he said, with some annoyance. "Client responsiveness means taking the client to lunch and listening to his needs of our firm. Every partner should know that."

The result of the MP's fixed idea was that, to nearly all the partners and the senior associates, the very idea of being more responsive to clients became something of a joke. The tragedy was that becoming more responsive was exactly what the firm needed, and if the MP had had the ability to listen to his partners' ideas of what it meant, he would have found some great suggestions of behaviors to adopt, and a great deal of support.

2. You are genetically predisposed to be a risk taker, or not

Risk takers are not generally aware that they are more willing to take a chance than others, and often are not able to take others' risk avoidance into consideration. Most leaders are risk takers; however, male leaders are generally more inclined to take risks involving the groups/firms they lead than female leaders.[5]

The board of a relatively large US firm had the job of finding a new CEO. The current holder of the post had been a consensus leader and had been inclined to take a "steady as she goes" approach to the challenges that he faced. Under his leadership, the business had grown steadily but without a great deal of innovation and there was a danger that other, more aggressive firms would begin to take a serious chunk of their market share.

The members of the board thought that a more dynamic leadership was called for and they decided – against our advice – to promote a man who had been the successful leader of one of their Asian branches. In that role, he had championed a number of innovations which the current CEO had thought too risky, and had vetoed.

As soon as he took the post, the new man began to make changes and to champion a merger with another firm of roughly the same size. He wouldn't listen to those partners advising caution, and who claimed that the merger target was not a good fit. His assumption, which he wouldn't allow to be challenged, was that the risk was worth it and the rewards should be self-evident to all but the most timid. He dismissed those who opposed him as being "too fearful" or "too near sighted". A number of his best rainmakers felt sidelined and left.

Within five months, the deal had collapsed and he himself left for another firm. "If I'd had more support", he intoned to us, "all would've been fine. They just didn't see it." Maybe, but the truth was that he couldn't see their point of view as valid. To him, such risk-taking was an essential part of leadership and it was that assumption that led to resistance and, ultimately, to failure.

Ask yourself: How often do you listen to, or read, the opinions of people you disagree with?

Assumptions based on experience

Of course, all stakeholders in any change situation have their own set of irrational assumptions; it is part of being human. Many of these are based on early experiences: childhood events, parental attitudes, teachers' and classmates' behaviors, and the like. Each of these can lead to assumptions that can render change more difficult for the individuals and the firm. Other assumptions can be based on work or other adult experiences.

Of course, not all assumptions are either harmful or wrong. Statistically, 30 percent are correct and even those that are not may be very useful in protecting the self from harm.

All assumptions – good or bad, right or wrong – are simply learned coping mechanisms. For example, a senior partner in a major Magic Circle firm in the UK had a parent who only praised her for her excellence at academic achievement. As a result, she was head of her class at school and in the top 0.5 percent of her class each year at law school. She got a job at the firm based on her deep knowledge of the law and her passion to explore it further. Her assumption was that her worth lay in her understanding of the intricacies of the law, for which she was praised and for which she was promoted. She was the firm's foremost expert in her field.

However, times change. Law firms change priorities. Flexibility, commerciality, and entrepreneurship became the watchwords for her firm. She feared the loss of importance that her grasp of the law had brought her. She couldn't change. She was sidelined. There are many lawyers like her in most firms whose assumptions about themselves prevent them from coming to terms with the changing needs of clients.

The more you try to persuade these lawyers of the need to change, the more they may become entrenched in their assumptions – no matter how many times they mouth their agreement. The reason for this is that our assumptions and our beliefs are very often so entrenched that they become part of our sense of self, and any attempt by someone to directly contradict them becomes, in our subconscious, an attack on us personally.

Overcoming resistance to change

However, as we said at the start, all is not lost. Humans do not like to change, but they can be persuaded to accept it, and recent discoveries in human science show how this can be done. Fear of social loss can be mitigated. Self-limiting assumptions, based on biology or experience, can be replaced by more enabling ones. But not by direct assault on a person's belief system or by giving them facts; both of these are often counter-productive.

In getting individuals or groups to change their behavior or their attitudes, there are two fundamental things to bear in mind and to act upon:

- Commitment to change is, in the end, commitment to you, or someone else, as a leader; and

- Commitment to lasting change can only be achieved if a person, or group, feels safe.

Getting commitment to you

The neuroscience of change is a hotly debated subject and is tied in with the whole issue of free will. Let's just say that the jury is out on some of the key issues. We do know a lot about the motivation and the process of change. All parties to the debate agree that people don't alter their behaviors or their attitudes because they have become persuaded by the facts or the reasoning. These are merely the excuses for the alterations, which happen after the decision to change has been made.[6]

Rather, people change their behaviors in order to strengthen actual, or potential, supportive relationships. They will adopt the new behaviors to gain the desired support, even if they do not necessarily believe in them. Whether the decision to alter a particular behavior or set of behaviors is ultimately conscious or unconscious, deliberate or automatic is irrelevant to this discussion – thank goodness!

We do know that if those new behaviors lead to good outcomes (ones where they are neurochemically gifted with one of the powerful reward neurochemicals, dopamine or oxytocin) then their brain (principally the orbitofrontal cortex, just behind the ear) will alter a person's "mindset" to account for, or justify, the behavioral change. This is true whether the change is a partner moving from one firm to another or their devoting more time and effort to business development.

As a firm leader, or as a manager or supervisor at any level of a firm who needs to promote changes in attitudes or behaviors, the relationship that most people need to be committed to is the one with you. If people feel that they will get more support and protection from you if they change their ways, then they will probably do so – even if they disagree with you.

The relationship that causes the change may be an existing relationship or a potential one. Often, you as a firm leader may be like a presidential candidate: a rather distant figure with whom most employees, even partners in large firms, will never have a real relationship. People can still develop a potential relationship with you, which can be just as effective in getting commitment.

People vote for politicians essentially because their striatum, a part of the limbic system of the brain that deals with trust and relationships (as well as a range of other things), has formed the opinion that the politician will offer them safety, and in order to gain that safety they will cast their vote in their favor. The striatum decides that there is a potential relationship between the voter and the candidate.

This decision can be based on a number of things that have little to do with what the politician stands for. It could be because they are taller than the other candidates (people tend to trust taller people), or has a deeper voice (people trust deeper voices more), or went to a similar school, or came from a similar town, or came from the same class, or is of the same race or gender, or has the same name, or has a combination of these or other commonalities which engender trust.

Having a similar world outlook can also be important, but having sufficient other commonalities can cause a person to vote for a candidate whose views they would not, initially, support. They will either change their views to rationalize the vote or argue that "really" they and the candidate share the same "values" or "outlook".

Having, and emphasizing, commonality is a vital way of gaining what we call "tribal commitment". However, in conjunction with other parts of the system, the striatum has other ways of judging the value of a real or potential relationship. You can inspire commitment to you, and to the change you advocate, through your actions or your achievements. Essentially, this is what a good role model does.

This action-inspiration is essentially a visual thing – something that is witnessed.[7] You are appealing directly to one of the most important social parts of the brain, where empathy lies – the mirror system. This is located in the left inferior frontal gyrus (at the front of the brain, just behind the eye).

Empathy with someone engenders commitment, and thus behavior change in order to support them – especially if there are commonalities in place. As with commonalities, the action or the modeling must be relevant to the person for them to be inspired. Just role modeling hard dedicated work will not inspire someone who doesn't feel that is the way for them. Scoring a hundred goals will not inspire somebody who hates football. A good leader will take the time to find out what actions will really inspire their followers, not just assume that they already know.

TOP TIP

What do you have in common with your workforce? How can you demonstrate it?

Looking for influencers

Over the last five years, it has been decided in marketing circles that one of the ways to get people to be aware of products is to get what are called "influencers" to promote them. A lot has been written on the subject, but little real research has been done. Influencers, the proponents of these marketing schemes assert, are leaders, just as you are.

The idea transferred to the workplace, and elaborate graphics are produced showing who is connected to whom. Those with the greatest number of connections are called the influencers. It is said that, collectively, they may have more influence in the firm than you have.

It has been estimated by Neil Farmer, in his rather infamous 2008 book, *The Invisible Organization*, that the top leadership – no matter how powerful the leaders are – has no more than 20 percent of the influencing ability available in the firm.[8] It makes sense, it would seem, to identify and convince these all-powerful influencers and have them work their magic on the rest of the firm.

However, recent research has cast a bit of cold water on the idea. The idea of influencers comes from marketing through social media. The marketers mapped the online networks of people and measured the clusters of contacts they had. Some subjects had many more significant contacts than others – more people read their posts, for example, or responded to their chats. By this means, the "influencers" spread information and, it was presumed, influence.

The idea spread to change programs in large businesses, including law firms. Convince the people that your partners and employees really listen to and all is well, the theory went. But, as a number of recent studies have shown, listening to and being influenced by are two quite different things. One of the more interesting findings of social media experts is that the so-called influence of influencers may be very short lived, certainly not long enough to change any ingrained behavior.[9] The other is that people tend to read the posts of people that they already agree with. In either case, no real change takes place.

The behavioral neurogenetic reason for this is simple: influencers may not be really or potentially part of people's support networks. People only change behavior to get closer to, or to appease, the nexus of those they want or need support from. The mass influencers are not tapping into that very powerful genetic driver that lies behind all real lasting change. This is not to say that mass influencers don't have some impact, only that it is brief and cannot be relied upon, except as a way of getting an initial message out.

The real influencers

For an individual partner or employee, real influencers are friends or support network members, or even people that they would like to have as part of their support network, not casual contacts. A leader can make use of this by instituting a mentoring program involving those in the firm that members admire or look up to – whether they are directly "connected" to them or not. Importantly, this must take into account differing cultural norms as to whom people admire, and not assumptions based on the leader's own social milieu. For example, in the US these influencers might be the chief rainmakers among the partners. Just over the border in Canada, they might not be so admired.

The firm leader should make a point of getting these people personally committed to them, and thus to any changes they want to institute. The real influencers become the change champions, the mentors, and the coaches. They will do this in order to solidify their relationship with the leader. In this way, adopting the new behaviors becomes the way that a person solidifies their place as a member of the firm's tribe.

Making change stick

Once people have made the commitment to a behavioral change, the trick is to make that change stick. There has to be an ongoing reward which the neurogenetic system recognizes. This system is extremely primitive and is common to all creatures that have a brain. It is also very, very powerful and is a key driver in almost all of our actions.

Technically, it is called the "mesolimbic dopamine reward system". It plays a vital role in keeping us functioning because it reinforces behaviors which, essentially, are good for us. Or rather, to be strictly accurate, were good for hunter-gatherers on the African savannah. When we do something which benefits either us personally or the group to which we belong, the nucleus accumbens (a part of the limbic system that controls the reward neurochemical dopamine) makes sure we feel a pleasurable sensation, or a sense of satisfaction. This reinforces the behavior which produced the reward. The actions become cemented as a habitual behavior in a part of the brain called the basal ganglia which stores these behaviors and directs many of our activities – such as the unconscious actions involved in driving a car to work.

As the famous Russian behaviorist Ivan Pavlov showed in the early years of the last century, the habit engrained by what we now know as a "dopamine reward" will remain even when the actual reward is withdrawn. This is the famous "Pavlovian reaction" or, more accurately, "classical conditioning". Although his theories and experiments have been refined many times since, they still form the basis of all behavioral change and learning theory.

The reward that makes new behaviors stick will vary from person to person and context to context – a reward that produces a change of behavior in your teenager might not work in the office, or vice versa. But although the particular rewards will vary, the most powerful ones fall into four specific categories. These are what we call the BASE (our own acronym) social drivers.[10] These are:

- Belonging;
- Acceptance;
- Status; and
- Self-esteem.

At first glance, some of these seem to be the same thing, but to the neurogenetic system they are crucially different.

Belonging
Belonging is the most powerful of all of the rewards, and has long been recognized as such.[11] As a hunter-gatherer, you could not survive outside of your supportive band; belonging was a life-or-death issue. Recent research has shown that most of our genetics are designed in some way to facilitate social belonging. We fear exclusion more than anything else – even death.[12] People need to feel that they belong to a mutually supportive tribe and you, as the leader, are the one to encourage this mutuality and offer belonging in return for specific behavior. In a hunter-gatherer band, observing the rituals and obeying the totems were the price of belonging. So it is with a modern law firm.

The most obvious manifestation of this is the set of "values" that most firms have instituted. The problem with many of these is twofold. Firstly, they do not come with a set of concrete behaviors that the partners, or others, are expected to abide by so they often become, like "client responsiveness" referenced above, or "excellence", effectively meaningless.

Secondly, often partners are seen to get away with not following them. This situation led the HR director of a major UK-based firm to tell us that the institution of values only showed up the toxic environment that existed in the business.

The behaviors associated with the values are the important factor, not the values themselves. When one large law firm we work with instituted a firm-wide behavioral charter based on the values of "trust", "respect", and "co-operation" (with a list of values, the fewer the better), management organized it so that the whole firm – from receptionists to senior partners – had a say in what the behaviors should be and a vote as to which ones should be put into the charter. A partner could not become a partner unless that individual subscribed to the values, and all existing partners were invited to sign, literally, onto the charter. Of 200 partners, 198 did so.

Social acceptance

Social acceptance is the visible sign that a person belongs to the tribe. As a leader, you show acceptance through praise, acknowledgement, or monetary reward. You noticeably show the person and others that you have accepted that individual, or group of individuals, into your circle of support, that they belong.

Again, in most firms there is some sort of ritual when lawyers are admitted into the partnership. The problem is that this type of ritual is usually limited to those becoming partners, not to non-lawyers being promoted or hired into the firm. This creates a "them and us" mentality. A functional hunter-gatherer band is organized to give all of its members a sense of being accepted. Often, partners defend the status-quo by saying that they are the "owners" of the business, or that they are the fee-earners and therefore deserve more acceptance than others.

Going forward, the first argument will be less and less true; most firms are being corporatized and, anyway, a sense of ownership when you have hundreds, if not thousands, of partners is wishful thinking. Such an organization is, in reality, no more than a joint-stock company (which, anyhow, many law practices are becoming) in which the partners are shareholders. The second point is also outdated. Recent research has shown that all the members of a firm contribute to its revenue, a point that is often overlooked and which we will be discussing later in the book.

Status

In a tribe status equals safety. We were on safari in Tanzania not long ago and one day, towards dusk, we witnessed the reaction of a pack of baboons to the approach of a pair of female lions on the hunt. The pack immediately ran to the nearest large tree and climbed up. Of course, the baboons knew, as we all do, that the big cats can climb trees. The interesting thing was that the higher status apes went to the top of the tree and the lower status ones were left with the lower branches, with the high possibility that they would be sacrificed to preserve the lives of those of superior status. Our guide informed us that this was how they normally arranged themselves at night.

Human packs are essentially no different, which is why a sense of status is so important to us. If we feel that we have some status within the organizational tribe, we feel we will be protected by the other members, especially by the tribal leadership. Many studies have shown that the need for social status is a major human driver. However, status does not necessarily equal rank or social position. An equal number have shown that the attainment of socioeconomic status, or hierarchical rank of themselves do not increase one's sense of life satisfaction. The sense of status that is important to human beings is relative to those immediately around you and with whom you have regular contact.[13]

If adopting a change of behavior leads to an increase in relative status, then the change will be more readily accepted. A respected leader like Gavin Bell, ex-managing partner of Freehills, or Cameron Jay Raines, joint CEO of DLA Piper, is someone we call "status rich". The respect, trust, and admiration that people have for such a leader gives them their status. As such, they are capable of bestowing status on others (you cannot give what you don't have). Usually, this is by giving their followers specific praise, public acknowledgement, or increased authority or autonomy.

We saw this in action at a US law firm where the CEO wanted to encourage his partners to form high-performing teams (HPTs) which would collaborate closely together and, to use his term, "hunt as a pack". Up until then, the partners had behaved more like, again to use his term, "sole practitioners sharing serviced offices", as is the case in many large US firms. With his senior management, he created a number of small, diverse teams of partners and associates and tasked them with:

- Seeking out new clients or reengaging old ones;
- Exploring and learning from the approaches that other firms had taken with those clients;
- Experimenting with these and other new business development approaches for those clients; and
- Exchanging knowledge they had gleaned with individual partners and other teams.

This strategy was not new or even rocket science, but it was a revolutionary tactic for his firm. He gave those teams that tried new and innovative ways of acquiring and retaining clients praise for their efforts and publicly acknowledged their innovations. The most successful teams were given added status as well as monetary reward. The result was increased income per partner over the firm as a whole as other teams learned from the successes of the best HPTs. They were similarly encouraged and rewarded, leading to a change in behavior throughout the firm.

Research conducted at the Big 4 accountancy firms has shown that when a partner or other employee is praised, acknowledged, or granted more autonomy by a respected leader, that person subconsciously creates for themselves what is known as an "identity script" in which they see themselves as having equal or more status than those around them. This solidifies the new behaviors that have allowed them to write the new script.[14]

Self-esteem

At first sight, a sense of status and self-esteem may seem much the same thing, but there are some fundamental differences. Firstly, status is totally bestowed upon us by outside influences such as our job title, the brand of the firm we work for, the praise and acknowledgement we are given. Self-esteem is largely hard-wired into us by our genes – maybe about 60 percent according to recent studies.[15] The neurophysiology of our brain, and in particular the strength of the signals that travel between the medial prefrontal cortex (the area dealing with self-knowledge) and the ventral striatum, also affects our level of self-esteem.[16]

In the end, probably 20 percent or so of our sense of self-worth comes from environmental influences. In behavioral terms, that is an important percentage. Essentially, a human's sense of self-esteem rises from its biological base when people make them feel good about themselves. These people could be a boss, family members, friends, clients, or co-workers. The interesting thing is that if this happens in one area of one's life, the feel-good factor is carried over into other areas. Within reason, the higher our level of self-esteem the more functional we are.

We all need a certain level of self-esteem in order to function without mental illness. A robust sense of self protects us from anxiety and depression and a number of other annoying psychiatric disorders (although too elevated a sense of self-esteem can be a sign of other pathologies). We tend to gravitate to those people, those firms, and those occupations that we believe will give us the most "bang for the buck" in self-esteem terms. And we will work hard to get it.

Increased self-esteem is undoubtedly a powerful motivator. So, what can you, as a law leader, do to use the drive to increase self-esteem among your partners and others in your firm? How can you frame rewards that add to commitment to new behaviors?

Firstly, you can increase the brand recognition of the firm. The greater the brand recognition, the more committed people will feel. Research has shown that people feel better, and are more productive, if they work for an organization that has a significant brand image. If your employees or partners believe that the new behaviors that you are advocating will lead to greater brand recognition, then that will trigger the reward mechanism of the brain and increase self-esteem. Secondly, you can demonstrate that the behavioral changes you advocate will lead to more accolades from clients, colleagues, the public, or even family members. All of these will use the drive for self-esteem to solidify the changes in behaviors and thus mindset that are necessary for the firm to prosper in the new reality.

TOP TIP

Think carefully about how you will reward behavioral change at the same time you decide on specific changes, and craft the two together.

Conclusion

We have discussed at length in this chapter the need to introduce and solidify behavioral changes. Of course, mere behavioral modifications are not enough to change the culture of a firm. But they are an essential start. Culture change, as we pointed out in the previous chapter, requires a change in mindset on the part of partners and employees.

The important take-away from this chapter is that mindset change is only possible as a result of the successful application of new behaviors. Mindset, in other words, is behaviorally based. The most dangerous thing a law leader can do is to assume that their partners and other employees will accept the need for change just because the law leader does. They won't. They will likely resist almost any changes that might impinge upon their nexus of supportive relationships.

The only way to successfully engineer change is to craft a series of rewards that will encourage people to attempt change and then put in place conditions that will inspire people to stick to those changes. The rewards and incentives must be in line with human neurogenetics, they must work with the grain of human nature and not, as with so many so-called incentives, against it.

References
1. Morris, P. and Halkitis, P., "The Influence of context on health", *Behavioral Medicine*, 41, 1–3, 2015.

2. Rosenblatt, Z. et al, "A Gender-based Framework of the Experience of Job Insecurity and Its Effects on Work Attitudes" *European Journal of Work and Organizational Psychology*, 8:2, 1999, pp. 197–217.

3. Avolio, B.J. et al, "The heritability of emergent leadership: Age and gender as moderating factors" *The Leadership Quarterly*, 23:2, 2012, pp. 219–232.

4. Fein, E. et al, "Cognitive basis for corruption and attitudes towards corruption in organizations viewed from a structuralist adult developmental meta-perspective", *Behavioral Development Bulletin*, 19:3, 2014, 78–94.

5. Ertac, S. et al, "Deciding to decide: Gender, leadership and risk-taking in groups" *Journal of Economic Behavior & Organization*, 83:1, 2012, pp. 24–30.

6. Stepien, R. et al, "Biologically inspired models of decision making" in *Advances in Cognitive Neurodynamics*, Springer Science, Drodrecht, 2015, pp. 55–56.

7. Goleman, D. and Boyatzis, R., "Social Intelligence and the Biology of Leadership", *Harvard Business Review*, September 2008.

8. Farmer, N., *The Invisible Organization*, Gower Publishing, Aldershot, 2008.

9. Krawczyk, J. and Steinberg, J., "How Content Is Really Shared: Close Friends, Not 'Influencers'", *Advertising Age*, 7 March 2012.

10. Serrat, O., A *Primer on Social Neuroscience Asian Development Bank*, Washington, DC, 2010.

11. Baumeister, R., "The need to belong: Desire for interpersonal attachments as a fundamental human motivation", *Psychological Bulletin*, 117:3, 1995, 497–429.

12. Baumeister, R. et al "Thwarting the Need to Belong: Understanding the Interpersonal and Inner Effects of Social Exclusion" *Social and Personality Psychology Compass*, 1:1, 2007, 506–520.

13. Anderson, C. et al, "The Local-Ladder Effect: Social Status and Subjective Well-Being" *Psychological Science* 23:7, 2012, pp. 764–771.

14. Bevort, F. and Suddaby, R., "Scripting professional identities: how individuals make sense of contradictory institutional logics", *Journal of Professions and Organization*, 2015.

15. Neiss, M. et al, "Genetic influences on level and stability of self-esteem" *Self and Identity* 5:3, 2006, pp. 247–266.

16. Chavez, R.S. and Heatherton, T.F., "Multimodal frontostriatal connectivity underlies individual differences in self-esteem", *Social Cognitive and Affective Neuroscience*, 10:3, 2015, pp. 364–370.

Chapter 7:
Building high-performing teams

This chapter will focus on:

- The science of ability and high performance;
- Creating high-performing teams;
- Inspiring high-performing teams; and
- The importance of high performance team dialogue.

"High performing" means many things in law firms. For a partner it can mean successful business development, but for other lawyers it can mean something else entirely, and something else again for non-legal staff. Indeed, as law firms change and morph, so will what is regarded as high performance. In this chapter, we look at high-performing teams (HPTs). These, too, will have different focuses as the firms themselves change. What is certain is that law firms will have to invest in creating high-performing teams that can innovate, adapt, and in doing so change the very nature of the business of law.

Whatever goals are set for them, and whatever their focus, there are certain basic characteristics that all HPTs possess, and certain ways in which they can be created. One thing to bear in mind at the outset is that a high-performing team is something special, very rare, and not at all like other kinds of teams. In our observations, few law firms have been successful in creating them.

The science of high performance

High intelligence (a high level of cognitive ability or IQ) is genetic in origin. Some people are simply more intelligent than others in this strict sense of the word. Like musical ability, cognitive ability tends to run in families.[1] This is true whether it is low or high intelligence. It has nothing to do with race, class, gender, or ethnicity, and the expression of intelligence (the way it manifests itself) will be largely a product of a person's environment. If an individual is in the highest echelon of intelligence (the top 5 percent) and, as a child, was given no way to express that intelligence because of parental attitude, socio-economic circumstances, race or gender expectations, and so forth, then they will not have the chance to become a high-performing individual in the intellectual sense of the word.

The same is, of course, true of other "intelligences", including emotional intelligence. This too is a trait that is genetic in origin and is highly heritable.[2] It is also part of high performance. Other traits connected with high performance have similarly been found to be encoded in individuals' DNA. These include endurance, attention to detail, ability to see the big picture, leadership, ability to deal with stress, calmness under pressure, ability to form strong working relationships, and so forth.

It is rare for any person to have more than a few of these traits at a very high level. There is an old phrase that "everyone is brilliant at something" which, it would seem from the latest research, is true at least to some extent. Very few people would seem to be born without the potential to be high performing at something.

When we talk of high performance in individuals, we are talking of someone who has a high level of one or more of the traits that enable them to perform a task, or a set of tasks, very well. A high-performing racehorse has to have stamina, speed, and an immune system that keeps it free from disease. These are all genetic traits, which is why champion horses are so in demand at stud. But the horse need not be particularly intelligent, or sociable, which are traits needed by a successful, and high-performing, partner in a legal practice!

A black-letter lawyer and one who is a rainmaker in the BD space may be quite different in their genetic make-up – which is why the two attributes rarely coexist in the same person. You can train a young lawyer who has the genetic potential to be a rainmaker to excel in bringing in clients, but it is much more difficult to turn the black letter lawyer into the rainmaker (or vice versa).

The other aspect of high performance that science has looked at is the desire to perform at one's peak. Having the right traits is of no use if you do not want to use them, or if you are not encouraged to do so. There is some evidence to show that the determination to succeed may be genetic,[3] but what is certain is that upbringing and work environment play a large part. Even if you have selected people for the right traits, you will not get high performance from them unless the environment within your firm encourages it.

Intelligence and determination are simply a collection of traits people have inherited; the expression of the DNA they were born with, moderated by the environment they were brought up in or which they find themselves in. A high-performing team is composed of people who have a number of these traits, but not necessarily the same ones. In fact, with two exceptions, it is much better if they do not share the same traits. Those exceptions are sociability and group (as opposed to individual) motivation. Some of these traits will probably not show up in an IQ test or even in a test for emotional intelligence.

The how-to of encouraging high performance is different in teams and in individuals, and a high-performing team is not necessarily composed entirely, or indeed at all, of high-performing individuals.[4] A high-performing team is composed of people who get their motivation to be high performing from being members of a mutually supportive team.

Creating high-performing teams

It is generally accepted that teams produce much better results than individuals do, whether that is in the area of strategy, sales, planning, or any other.[5] What is also widely accepted is that really high-performing teams are very rare.[6] (In over 20 years as corporate consultants, we have seen maybe a dozen or so.)

However, as my colleagues and I have demonstrated in numerous firms, creating and inspiring HPTs is possible within the law firm context. HPTs are an essential ingredient, for example, in the successful implementation of change and other strategies, and one of the reasons why so many fail is that the teams charged with implementing them are much less than high performing.[7]

Though there is no commonly accepted definition of a high-performing team, according to team creation guru Glenn Parker, author of the book *Team Players and Teamwork*, there are 12 essential characteristics of a high-performing team: clear purpose, informality, participation, listening, civilized disagreement, consensus decision, open communication and trust, clear roles and work assignments, shared leadership, external relations, style diversity, and self-assessment.[8] In our experience, most teams in law firms lack many of these features.

We recently worked with the National Leadership Team (NLT) of a prominent law firm in New York. When we started working with them, the firm was going through the process of merging with another firm of roughly the same size and the NLT was overseeing the process – not very successfully. In meetings, the 15-member team engaged in lengthy, unproductive debate. Each made statements in support of their own point of view, that of their teams, or their practice areas. There was no indication that they were really listening to each other – except to score points off each other. There was no questioning to show the slightest curiosity as to how their colleagues had come to particular positions. There was no sign of what Parker would call "civilized disagreement"; the disagreement was often quite uncivilized. Nor was there any sign of consensus decision making or new ideas coming to the fore. Decisions were made by the CEO regardless of what anybody said. All the benefits of working as a team were lost.

We have seen many "teams" like the one in the case study above in action. The question is: how do you get from a firm that has those kinds of teams to one that has genuinely high-performing teams?

First off, the New York team was much too large. Recent research has shown that the ideal team size is six or seven. Professor Katherine Kline of the Wharton School of management notes: "There is a sense that as a team gets larger, there is a tendency for social loafing, where someone gets to slide, to hide."[9] When that happens, the value of having a team gets lost and the possibility of it becoming an HPT is gone.

Diversity in HPTs

There are two main theories about diversity in HPTs. One theory, advanced by Kline, is that it is better to have a majority of people who share similar mental models in a team – people who think in the same way, and have a lot of commonality in their outlook on life. They may share similar backgrounds, or be of the same or similar ethnicity. Other researchers think that diversity is perhaps the cornerstone of a high-performing team.

Parker mentions "style diversity" as being important, but more recent research has shown that diversity of style is only one aspect of diversity and, though important, is by no means the most important aspect of it. For example, a 2013 survey by Ernst & Young found that teams that had more diversity were more successful in becoming HPTs.[10] In fact, the more diversity the better. Still another study, published in 2015, showed that even diversity in mood was beneficial to team performance, provided that there were a number of team members who had sufficient emotional intelligence to recognize, direct, and moderate the different mood states.[11]

We think these two positions can be reconciled by looking scientifically at the way human beings actually operate. People are genetically predisposed to cooperate better with those who we perceive to be members of our own tribe. However, as recent studies of hunter-gatherer tribes has shown, this similarity has little if anything to do with kinship. Rather, the essence of a tribe is commonality. If there is enough commonality, there will be inclusion. Research shows that inclusiveness rather than just diversity is what is essential.

Commonality simply means having a number of things in common. It is one of the main hallmarks of trust; the more you and I have in common, the more we will see each other as real or potential members of the same tribe, and the genetic predisposition to cooperate with each other will kick in. A skilled leader will therefore emphasize the things that people who follow them have in common and, right from the start, give them ample opportunity to socialize and discover even more things that they have in common. The opportunity to exchange what used to be called "idle gossip" is now globally recognized as one of the most important parts of the creation of an HPT.[12]

Any HPT must be composed of people who trust and respect each other – that's fairly obvious. More than that, they must actually like each other.[13] A number of studies have shown that this "liking" is perhaps the most important aspect of an HPT. It seems to be much more important than having a team composed of high-performing individuals who, because of ego-clashes, are rarely high performing as a group.

TOP TIP

Make sure your teams have a diversity of background, gender, and outlook.

Virtual HPTs

Even rarer than an ordinary HPT is a virtual one. The reason for this is the very human need for regular face-to-face communication. It is one of the essential elements of creating and maintaining trust.

Most major law firms are in the process of trying to create virtual teams, whether these are of lawyers, business development professionals, or learning and development specialists. In our experience, few of these actually work well and the main reason for this, we believe, is lack of trust. The firms are simply not putting the investment into bringing the teams together on a regular basis.

An example of this was the business development team of a top 50 US firm. We had been working with the team leaders for a while when the firm suddenly slammed down a cost-saving initiative severely restricting travel for non-partners. Even travelling between Boston and Miami became a problem, let alone Sydney, Hong Kong, or London. Very quickly, the members of the BD leadership team – who were spread around the world – began to lose trust in each other, communication became more electronic and formal, and a sharp division between the staff at firm headquarters and the rest became evident.

Almost all of this would have been avoided if the team had been given the chance to get together more often to exchange information in an informal setting. As Parker claims, it is face-to-face communication in an informal setting that enables a true exchange of really worthwhile information and experience. Perhaps one day we will have the technology to be able to recreate all the senses involved in face-to-face communication virtually, but until then even virtual teams will have to meet often to become HPTs.

TOP TIP

You cannot have a virtual high-performing team if they cannot get together regularly.

Key points for creating an HPT
In short, to create an HPT a leader must:

- Keep the team small – between three and seven individuals;
- Make it diverse in terms of background, gender, and style;
- Be sure that they encourage commonality and inclusion;
- Choose people who get along with each other;
- Allow time for social mixing; and
- Make sure that even virtual team members frequently get together in person.

The role of the firm leader

There is no such thing as a "leader" of an HPT and the worst thing that you can do is appoint one. Yet that's just what most firm leaders do. Worse, they often try to make themselves the leaders of HPTs. Having the boss on the team is a bad idea because no matter how egalitarian the firm, or division, or department leader is, they are still "the boss" and will, at least subconsciously, be judging individual performance rather than team effectiveness. It is also obvious that the other members of the team will defer to the boss. A firm leader's best management style with an HPT is laissez-faire – set the goals and waypoints (the stages) for checking in and then stand back and let them get on with it.

Leadership in an HPT will vary from project to project and between phases within a project. In the best teams, leaders for particular stages of a project will emerge rather than be appointed.[14]

So, what then is the role of the firm, division, or department leader? There are four primary roles:

- Set objectives. Before you even create the team, work out clearly what the objective of the team is. For any team to function at its best it must have a clear mission. The mission must be meaningful to the members and one that gives them a sense of purpose.

- Facilitate dialogue. Once the team has been established and the members understand their mission, help them to clarify and agree how they will work together. This does not mean laying down the law; rather, at this early stage, it means facilitating their dialogue.

- Agree goals and way-points. Agree with the members of the team the near-term goals that you need them to achieve and the way-points at which you want them to check in with you to confirm that all is on course. It is important that they let you know if they are not going to meet these way-points at the time agreed. It is amazing how many leaders in law firms ignore this very simple rule.

- Inspire the team. This is the most important part of your role (for more on this see Chapter 3).

The importance of high performance team dialogue

Peter Senge, one of the foremost theorists of the art of dialogue, drew a sharp distinction between discussion and dialogue. In discussion, he said, people take and hold positions, like in a debate; in dialogue, people suspend their positions and probe others for their reasoning to discover new possibilities.[15]

One of the key features of good team dialogue is that it should contain more positive than negative phrases and words. A rule of thumb is that the ratio of positive statements to negative ones should be at least 3:1. Really top HPTs have been observed to achieve a ratio of something like 10:1.[16]

Based on the work of Senge and his collaborator Otto Scharmer, and our own 20 years of watching and listening to high- and low-performing teams, we have come up with a model (see Figure 1) of how teams can move from being low performing to high performing, and how they can change from rather low-intensity (in terms of results) to high-intensity dialogue.

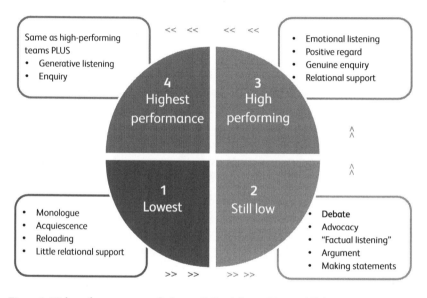

Figure 1: High performance team dialogue, © Fortinberry Murray 2016

The discussions in almost all of the teams in law firms that we have encountered fall into the first two categories. In fact, we have rarely encountered a team in a law firm that dialogued *consistently* in the top two categories. Admittedly, those in the fourth category are rare indeed in any organization.

It is the job of any law leader wanting to set up HPTs in their firm to make sure that the teams do not get stuck in the first two categories. Most of the terms in the categories are obvious, but several are not quite so. What is "reloading" (category 1), for example? You are reloading when you are thinking of your answer or your riposte while the other person is still talking. It is one of the main reasons that we do not really hear about 40 percent of what people are saying.[17] Many teams get stuck in the reloading rut because the members are only prepared to hear that which confirms their own assumptions and beliefs. Nothing new can get in.

Once a team gets to the second level, they have made some improvement, and the reason is that they are doing what Scharmer calls "factual listening". It is the (somewhat rare) ability to switch off your judgment and listen to the facts that another person is presenting, even if they go against your own assumptions and beliefs. Listening in this way is called object-focused: the listener is paying attention to facts and to novel or disconfirming data.

The judgment that you switch off is the inner censor lodged in the orbitofrontal cortex where our assumptions and beliefs reside. We tend not to hear or remember information which contradicts our belief system, and when we do we tend to "reframe" it in such a way that it actually supports our assumptions. Using factual listening, you focus on what differs from what you already know. It is the basic mode of good science. You ask questions, and you pay careful attention to the responses you get.

The dialogue of real HPTs is in the third and fourth segments of the model. The key to getting to the third stage is the ability to get out of your own head and away from your own agenda. You listen not only for facts, but for feelings – the hopes and fears that others have which lie behind the facts they want to impart. It's what we call "emotional listening". You engage the right supramarginal gyrus, part of the mirror neuron system, which allows us to get into the head and emotions of other people. You listen with empathy. You also listen to the particular words that the other person is using, which often signal their emotions, and based on these ask questions to discover hidden assumptions or feelings which might be behind the positions they take.

It is strange but true that in work situations we rarely ask people about their feelings – thoughts yes, but emotions no. When you really begin to understand another person's feelings you are listening not just to ideas or thoughts, but also to feelings and emotions. It is listening, as Scharmer says, with an "open heart".

At this level, a team will also be using more positive than negative language. We have noticed that one of the things that distinguishes all low-performing teams – like the NLT that we mentioned earlier – are the number of negative statements and phrases that are used. We counted the number of positive and negative comments during one of their meetings and the result was 57 negative and 16 positive.

There were numerous comments such as "Oh! We've tried that before and it didn't work!", "That's a really crazy idea!", or "That would never work!". In an HPT, these phrases would be banned. Rather, the correct way of approaching an idea that you do not agree with is not to shoot it down. It is to find out what is behind it, what the person who put it up is really interested in, what their fears are, and so forth.

So you say: "That's an interesting idea. I'm curious to know how you got to that." You are making a positive statement, and you are going on to show that interest through what is called "appreciative enquiry". You may find that there is the kernel of something really worthwhile that you would not have found if you had dismissed the idea out of hand.

In appreciative enquiry you help the person, and the rest of the team, to become more aware of the underlying issues behind the comment or statement. What are the person's assumptions, hopes, and fears? It may be that uncovering these can lead the person to identifying needs that must be met before the issue at hand can be resolved. When they are, the team can then find a new way forward together.

Members of an HPT have a high level of positive regard for each other and this is clear by the way they demonstrate respect for each other and their ideas. This does not mean that you can never make a negative comment. They are inevitable in the course of conversations even within an HPT. Probably, most of the comments that are made will be neutral and it would be perfectly fine to approach the dialogue above by leaving out the fact that you find the idea "interesting" if you really don't. In that case, you would go straight to "I'm curious to know how you arrived at that".

Since HPTs in law firms are usually formed in a culture where praise of any sort is rare at first, this emphasis on the positive in dialogue will have to be practiced. It may well be met with eye-rolls until the practice of emphasizing the positive, and avoiding the putdown, becomes normal.

Since members of an HPT have a high positive regard for each other, it is only natural that they will show each other a high degree of relational support. Indeed, it is this that is the primary reason for their success. A team will strive for excellence because of it. They become a tribe whose existence depends on their ability to perform at a high level.[18]

In many ways, hunter-gatherer hunting bands were the best of all HPTs and exhibited all of the characteristics that Parker and others have noted. We believe that the drive for excellence in support of those we rely on is a genetic trait of many species that hunt in packs, as dogs do. This is most particularly true of humans because we rely on the support of others for our survival far more than others do. On the savannah, a lone lion can and does survive on its own, but a human cannot do so for very long.

At the very top – the highest, and very rarest, of HPTs – are those that can practice what Scharmer calls "generative listening", together with what we call "generative inquiry". To Scharmer, when the team engages in "generative listening" it has gone beyond individuals and is listening "from the emerging field of the future". Together, the team is connected to a deeper source of knowing. Possibilities can open up and profound change is possible. It is what Boyatzis calls "brain to brain transmission" involving the motor-neuron circuit. It activates attention in ways that allow the team to be open to new ideas and new emotions.[19]

Generative enquiry is a means whereby the people in the team use questioning to engage each other to come up with something new. By not accepting any answer as the final one but constantly probing deeper, the prefrontal cortex has to rearrange itself to innovate, to stop listening to the censor, to stop putting full stops at the end of thoughts, and to see each as a new beginning. In generative inquiry, there are no final answers. The team may choose to stop at a particular place because in reaching it they have resolved the problem at hand, but at this level of performance they know that there is another innovation beyond the one that they have found and that this is a process without end.

We are frequently asked how long a really high-performing team should be kept together. Our answer is "forever".

Listen to the dialogue of all your teams and decide which are really high performing, and take action to disband or upskill those that are not.

Conclusion

An HPT is not an ordinary team, nor is it a team made up exclusively of high-performing individuals. It tends to be diverse, literally "leaderless", and with its own distinct dialogue patterns. It is a rarity in most law firms, but one to be carefully created and nourished.

Law leaders find it a difficult beast to manage because it is often hard for them to stand back and allow for a more laissez-faire style of leadership than they are used to. In many ways, it is more like a gathering of friends than a work team – the work is the excuse for the gathering. There's often a lot of laughter because, essentially, they are having fun. The dopamine gets flowing and their brains begin to work faster, and more creatively. The firms that can become a network of HPTs are the ones that will survive through the 21st century.

References

1. Shakeshaft, N. et al, "Thinking Positively: The genetics of high intelligence" *Intelligence*, 48, 2015, pp.123–132.

2. Petrides, P. et al, "A behavioral genetic study of trait emotional intelligence" *Emotion*, 8:5, 2008, pp.635–642.

3. Timmermans, S., "The genetics of determination", talk detailing studies on the topic delivered 20 October 2014 at UCLA.

4. Yates, D.E. and Hylen, C. *High Performing Self-managed Work Teams*, Sage Publications, London, 1997.

5. See further Heffernan, M., *Beyond Measure: The Big Impact of Small Changes*, TED Books, New York, 2015.

6. Castka, P. et al, "Factors affecting successful implementation of high performance teams", *Team Performance Management: An International Journal*, Vol. 7:7/8, 2001, pp.123–134.

7. Hoag, B. et al, "Obstacles to effective organizational change: the underlying reasons", *Leadership & Organization Development Journal*, 23:1, 2002, pp.6–15.

8. Parker, G., *Team Players and Teamwork*. 2nd Edition, Jossey-Bass, San Francisco, 2008.

9. Kline, K. et al, "Team mental models and team performance", *Journal of organizational Behavior*, 27, 2006, pp.403–418.

10. Ernst & Young, "Characteristics of High Performing Teams" *Global Review*, 2013; available at www.ey.com/GL/en/About-us/Our-global-approach/Global-review/global-review-2013-building-high-performance-teams#page1.

11. Collins, A. et al, "Positive affective tone and team performance: The moderating role of collective emotional skills", *Cognition and Emotion*, 30:1, 2015, pp.167–182.

12. For example, see Manaf, A. et al "Gossip Has It! An In-Depth Investigation of Malaysian Employees on Gossip Activities at Workplace", *Canadian Social Science*, 9:4, 2013, pp.34–44.

13. Pentland, A., "The New Science of Building Great Teams" *Harvard Business Review*, July 2012.

14. Stagl, K.C. et al, "Best Practices in Team Leadership", in Jay Conger and Ronald Riggio (eds.), *The Practice of Leadership*, Jossey-Bass, San Francisco, 2007, pp.172–197.

15. Senge, P., The Fifth Discipline, *The Art and Practice of the Learning Organization*, Doubleday, New York, 1990, Chapter 12.

16. Cameron, K. et al, "Effects of Positive Practices on Organizational Effectiveness" *Journal of Applied Behavioral Science*, 47:3, 2011, pp.266–308.

17. Gunnlaugson, O., "Shedding Light on the Underlying Forms of Transformative

Learning Theory", *Journal of Transformative Education*, 5:2, 2007, pp.134–151.

18. Michaelsen, L. et al, "Beyond Groups and Cooperation: Building High Performance Learning Teams" in *To Improve the Academy: Resources for Faculty, Instructional, and Organizational Development*, New Forums Press, Stillwater, 1993, pp.127–145.

19. Boyatsis, R., "Neuroscience and the Link Between Inspirational Leadership and Resonant Relationships", *Ivy Business Journal*, January/February, 2012.

Chapter 8:
The art and science of effective persuasion

This chapter covers:

- Why reasons and facts do not persuade people;
- The science of persuasion;
- Mutual satisfaction of needs and persuasion;
- The SCARF persuaders;
- Nonverbal persuasion techniques; and
- The 10 commandments of persuasion.

One managing partner recently expressed some frustration to us: "The changes I'm suggesting are so obviously essential for the success – perhaps the very survival – of our firm. Almost all of our successful competitors have already transferred to a far more robust performance-based REM and are instituting similar shifts in support services and technology. But you'd think I was asking partners to hand over their first-born child!"

This sentiment was echoed by a newly-appointed BD head of a large multinational law firm at a recent get-together of law firm leaders: "When I first came here I had great ideas about how I would persuade the partners to adopt some of the very successful business development strategies that my team and I had developed for the partners of the firm I last worked for. It didn't work out that way. The partners were very nice to me, very friendly, but made it perfectly plain, by their actions and behavior, that they had no intention of changing their ways." The conclusion of all members of the get-together was that, if partners of this or any other similar established firm did not change their ways, there was no long-term future for them.

Every day you set out to persuade people, to get them to see your point of view, to "get them onside". Sometimes, you succeed – and sometimes you fail. Overwhelmingly, the people you "persuade" are those who agreed with you in the first place, at least on a subconscious level. Leadership, in law or any other business, is about persuading people – often to do that which they do not consciously or subconsciously agree with. This is especially true in a rapidly shifting environment when the leader must institute changes which people – partners, lawyers, and support staff – will find uncomfortable or even painful.

As we say in Chapter 1, selling your services is about persuading actual or potential clients that you are an indispensable part of their support network, despite the myriad of other services available. So, what is effective persuasion? In this chapter, we will look at how law leaders must persuade their people to change. We will present a case that persuasion is quite different from what people used to think it was. Recent research in neurophysiology and neurogenetics has uncovered the real brain and genetic pathways of persuasion. We will also show you some effective persuasion tools.

Why reasons and facts do not persuade people

"The king is not persuaded by your reasoning!" This pithy comment was written 2,500 years ago in Babylonic cuneiform on a tablet unearthed as a result of an American bombing raid on Iraq in 2003. It sums up current knowledge of the power of cognitive reasoning in persuasion: it has none.

As scientists, we are frequently amused when we watch law leaders, partners, and others trying to persuade people. Almost immediately, they begin by setting out the facts supporting their arguments. This is, after all, what they were trained to do. The idea is that if you give people the facts, or at least selected facts, they will see your point of view, and they will be persuaded.

The traditional model of persuasion is based on the belief that when people are given facts they draw conclusions based on them. The conclusions may be accurate or inaccurate, but they are based on that which is verifiable. Skilled persuasion would consist of marshaling selected facts and showing how they led, inescapably, to the conclusion you want the individual to come to. You could bolster your case with cogent reasoned arguments drawn from those facts.

This seems reasonable and, until very recently, it was assumed that this was the way to do it. Our legal system is based on this theory and so was our system of economics. However, the human system does not actually work that way. In fact, persuasion is largely about neither truth nor facts but, like any other decision process, about emotions and being a member of the person's tribe.

Increasingly, people are turning to the behavioral model adopted in many fields such as economics. This model assumes that because of the power of our assumptions and our unwillingness to let go of them, persuasion is the art of showing that your arguments are actually aligned with, and perhaps will strengthen, another person's beliefs. As two Harvard professors pointed out in a now-famous working paper, as a persuader it does not matter if your facts are correct or not, or whether they are relevant to the matter at hand. What matters is that they fit in with the assumptions and beliefs of the person you are trying to persuade.[1] This commonality makes you part of the same tribe and therefore more trustworthy.[2]

The professors give the example of Alberto Culver Natural Silk Shampoo, which contained some silk, and was advertised with a slogan: "We put silk in a bottle". The idea was obviously to suggest that the product makes hair silky, even though the company spokesman conceded that "silk doesn't really do anything for hair". The marketer's aim was to benefit from the audience's belief that it was important to have "silky" hair in order to be attractive and accepted in the community and, perhaps, their commonsense, but erroneous, assumption that silk would make hair "silky".

In the behavioral model, far from trying to convince the audience that it holds erroneous beliefs, the persuader attempts to benefit from such beliefs. And, like the need to have "silky hair", the belief can be cultural as well as personal. You convince few people if you attack the beliefs embedded in their culture. Saying that "silky" hair is not the same as healthy hair will get you nowhere if the person feels they will have less chance of exclusion if they have hair like silk.

In the competition between truth – given in facts, surveys, and studies – and deeply held belief, belief will win every time. It may be intellectually satisfying to marshal the facts to disprove a person's assumptions, but it is futile as a method of persuasion. (However, as with the silky hair example, you can use this belief-bias to your advantage!)

A rather neat example of this came in a workshop given at a large law firm not long ago. Bob gave as an example of evidential bias the 2014 Gallup Poll which showed that 42 percent of people in the US still believe in creationism despite all the evidence to the contrary. Unfortunately, one of the most senior partners present was one of those deniers. He was also the one being the most truculent, disputing many of the things being said. The almost overwhelming temptation was for Bob to seize on this and give a quick summary of the evidence for evolution – to "prove" that the partner's belief was wrong. But he took a different, more persuasive tack.

He acknowledged that the partner had made a good point, and agreed that there are many aspects of classical Darwinian theory which are erroneous. The man nodded his head in a satisfied manner. Bob also acknowledged that there are now many quantum physicists who say that it is impossible to conceive of the universe without some form of creator, which resulted in a broad grin on the face of the partner. "It may be that we are in violent agreement on many things", said Bob, holding out his hand for a shake.

For the rest of the workshop the partner was clearly onside and, indeed, recommended that the session be given to all the firm's partners. While not pretending to agree with a view contrary to his own, Bob affirmed the partner in his core beliefs and therefore showed that he was not a threat. The man was now open to persuasion on the more non-core assumptions covered in the workshop.

It's not that your facts are irrelevant, they are not. But they are not persuasive.

The science of persuasion

Human beings have no neural mechanism that allows us to be persuaded by facts alone. Rather, we are persuaded by the amount of two neurochemicals (oxytocin and dopamine) that get to the decision-making parts of the brain.

Persuasion goes through the same neural pathways as relationships. In fact, the two are intrinsically linked. Persuasion is essentially about showing that you are, actually or potentially, part of a person's support network. People are predisposed to persuasion by their need for support and the belief that you can deliver it. Their "acceptance" of what you say is a way of subconsciously buying your support, whether they really believe what you say or not.

That acceptance happens very quickly through chemical information going to the relational/trust/emotional part of the brain and then to the "action" areas of the brain, leading them to do as you suggest. Recent research has shown that the same area that regulates trust and relationships, the striatum, is also the major seat of action (more on the striatum will follow below).[3] The neural process of being persuaded begins deep in what were once seen as the most primitive parts of the brain, which include both the striatum and the amygdala. All data – whether through words, senses, or even memories – coming into the human system goes through the amygdala. This is in that part of the cortex called the limbic system, or what used to be known as the "reptilian brain" because we share it with crocodiles. Now we know it is really part of a wider system that we share with every creature that has a brain.

The job of this walnut-shaped area at the base of the skull is to keep us safe and prepare us for immediate action if it perceives danger. The amygdala is not very clever, but it is extremely quick. According to many neuroscientists, it operates at the speed of 40 nanoseconds – 40 billionths of a second. In that time it decides – in conjunction with a couple of other nearby areas of the brain – whether or not to trigger the sympathetic nervous system.

The sympathetic nervous system's task is to trigger the release of stress hormones such as cortisol, which ready the body to fight, flee, or freeze. In cases of perceived strong danger (say, during a negative performance review) the amygdala may take total control of the brain and nervous system in what Daniel Goleman, author of the book *Emotional Intelligence* calls an "amygdala hijack".[4] If this happens, no relationship will be formed and no persuasion is possible.

What triggers the amygdala to galvanize the sympathetic nervous system? The main human-generated triggers are:

- A frown at the beginning of an interaction;
- Criticism at any time (criticism is very different from constructive, if negative, feedback);
- Any real or implied threat;
- A situation that is similar to a threat from the past;
- A statement that implies a danger to one's sense of status;
- Perceived lack of personal control; and
- Seeing someone else threatened, bullied, or abused.

There are ways to make sure that the amygdala is co-operative. These are:

- Give the person specific praise – if you are valued, you are less likely to be rejected;
- Make a statement upfront implying that you want the relationship to continue;
- Begin with a smile – the age-old signal that you mean no harm;
- Offer a warm handshake – originally, this demonstrated you had no weapon, but we now know it carries important persuasion signals to the cortex;[5]
- Accentuate commonalities – show you are a member of their tribe;
- Offer food (ask them to a meal or coffee);
- Respect their boundaries (especially, keep a polite physical distance);
- Show genuine interest in them or their interests or concerns; and/or
- Confirm some aspect of their assumptions – people identify themselves with their beliefs and will perceive an attack on these as a threat to their sense of self.

These actions demonstrate that someone is a "friend" and put the amygdala at ease. The data is then allowed to proceed to the relationship/trust/emotion part of the brain centered on the striatum. The striatum is the trust and relationship core of the brain. If the striatum receives a strong "safe" signal from the amygdala, it prepares to release (in conjunction with the reward system center of the brain, the nucleus accumbens) two of the most powerful neurochemicals in the human system: dopamine, the reward neurochemical, and oxytocin. Oxytocin is the bonding and trust substance – without it mothers would not bond with their offspring and business deals would never get done.

Effectively, the striatum makes a judgment call. It asks: Is this person really or potentially part of my supportive relationship nexus? If the safe signal it receives is really strong, the striatum sends signals using oxytocin and dopamine to the nearby caudate nucleus, an area of the brain recently shown to have important functions in memory and learning. Some have called it the decision center of the brain. It is also the bonding and romantic love center of the brain. So, in this striatum/

caudate area, learning, bonding, and executive action all come together. This nucleus is the target of persuasion.

The caudate is persuaded by the strength of the dopamine and oxytocin signal coming from the striatum. Effectively, it is making up its mind to accept whatever the persuader says or suggests in order to create a new relationship or strengthen an existing one with that person. In the process, it commits the new data regarding the relationship to memory, creates a bond, and together with the striatum, commits the system to action. The caudate itself reinforces the flow of dopamine to make sure that the person being effectively influenced feels that doing the suggested action feels virtuous, rewarding, or pleasurable.[6]

Of course, during the conversation – or the interaction – the skilled persuader will periodically use praise and make relationship statements, both of which are powerful dopamine producers. They will ask questions to draw out commonalities, thus stimulating oxytocin. They will smile and nod to reinforce safety. All of this will keep the other person's brain attentive, receptive, and attuned to the message. If the signals are strong enough, the striatum/caudate decision to accept and action the persuader's message will be sent to the prefrontal cortex – the area just behind the eyes where the conscious mind is located – for ratification. The prefrontal cortex will seek out or manufacture reasons or excuses for accepting the influencer's thoughts, ideas, or suggestions. This is the final stage of persuasion.

Your facts do not have to be correct, but the way you present them must be.

Persuasion and needs

The persuasion pathway is not always all that is needed, especially if you need to influence someone not just once but frequently over a period of time. For that, you need to create more of an enduring trust-based relationship.

For a person to have confidence in you over the long term, they must trust you. (You must use all of the five elements of trust mentioned in Chapter 9.) In addition, you must be able to show that you can meet their needs. After all, any relationship, as we have said before, is based on the mutual satisfaction of need. And to do this you must demonstrate that you are competent to do so. This isn't about touting your superior wisdom and CV. It is about finding out what their needs are and honestly exploring how you might meet them. You must also be prepared to help the other party to understand your needs of them. A relationship is a mutual satisfaction of need, and in many ways these mutual needs are the rules of the relationship.

For people to feel safe, they need to believe that they know the rules of the relationship with you and can be confident that the relationship is secure if they follow those rules. This is just as true of your clients as it is of the people who work for and with you.

The important thing about needs is that they must be concrete, actionable, and time specific. We often tend to express our needs of people couched in general terms: "I need you to respect me", or "I need you to be a better team player", or even "I need this ASAP". All of these are meaningless in terms of anything that the hearer can actually do to meet them. They have to guess at your meaning, and this leads to anxiety since often they will be wrong.

The need must be about performing an action rather than perception or emotion. "I need you to take this on board" is a pointless request since the brain cannot do it on command. Rather, ask yourself what you would like to see a person do if they had "taken it on board" and ask for those actions. Similarly, with requests for emotions such as "love", "respect", and so forth. Finally, without some sort of time frame the expression of any need is pointless.

The exchange of needs helps people to become invested in the relationship with you. Their brains will be more open to do what you suggest – to be persuaded – in order to solidify the relationship. In fact, they will get an oxytocin and dopamine hit every time they meet one of your needs.

Advanced persuading – Using SCARF
Once you have opened the brain to persuasion, the next trick is to frame what you want to say in ways that have the most chance of continuing success. In 2008, David Rock published an article in the *Neuroleadership Journal* about what he saw as the five drivers of human behavior, which he collectively called SCARF. These are the need for status, certainty, autonomy, relatedness, and fairness.[7] This model has since become something of a celebrity in management circles.

The idea is that the human brain is wired to seek to increase each of these and will be persuaded to behave in ways that seem to make maximizing them possible. If someone believes that public recognition from the boss will increase their status in the eyes of those they want to impress, then they will do what it takes to get that recognition. Suggesting to them that certain actions will lead to getting the desired recognition will be a powerful persuader. The same is true of all the five elements of the model. The other interesting thing about Rock's findings is that, to some extent, the elements are interchangeable.

An example of SCARF in action occurred in a large UK law firm we worked with recently. The leadership of the firm decided to virtually eliminate the firm's HR department and to either digitize or outsource the necessary but more routine functions. The partners in the business would have to do many of the higher-level HR functions connected with the running of their teams themselves. These included deciding on staff leave and organizing their teams' training programs. The partners saw this as a diminution of their status as this work had typically been done by people they saw as of lower rank than themselves. They also saw it as unfair – they already felt overburdened by the need to fulfill their billable hours quota and do their business development.

The firm's leadership approached the job of persuading the partners to accept the new arrangement with SCARF in mind. They were taking away elements of both status and fairness and these had to be replaced with increased emphasis on the remaining three drivers. They talked up the fact that the move would give the partners much more autonomy in a range of areas, such as allocating staff leave at times to suit the work-flow and the kind of training and coaching that their teams needed. They emphasized the fact that the new arrangements would strengthen the relationships between partners and their teams since they would have to work together more closely on issues which they had previously left to HR. Finally, they showed that the partners would have certainty, going forward, that there would be no more changes.

So far, with the exception of a few grumbles, the new arrangements are working out well. It was a good exercise in persuasion.

Of course, SCARF can be used in many areas. Persuading a new client to hire the services of you or your firm is much easier if you can show them that your representing them will lead to an increase in their status in the eyes of those that they care about (their board or their CEO, for example), their sense of certainty about the outcome, their freedom of action, and so on.

Research has shown that these are, in fact, very powerful drivers, and they are very useful as a way of planning an approach to persuasion. They cannot, with the possible exception of the relatedness element, be relied upon on their own. No one will be persuaded by cognitive reasoning alone, since the brain simply does not work that way.[8]

Other nonverbal persuaders

Over 50 percent of our communication is nonverbal, so it is hardly surprising that nonverbal persuasion techniques can be very powerful. The reason is that they, too, can trigger the brain's reward system and also lead to other physiological benefits which open the brain to influence. The following is a by-no-means-exhaustive list of some of the main nonverbal influencing techniques you can use on a daily basis:

- Take the person you want to influence to lunch or any meal. Besides oxytocin and dopamine, a neurochemical that will help you win people over is glutamate. In the gut, glutamate breaks down food as an essential part of metabolism. Glutamate in the brain acts as a neurotransmitter involved in memory and learning. Studies have shown that we are more open to being influenced just after we have eaten and this is due to another of glutamate's actions. It causes the brain to relax and to see the world in a more optimistic light. When calm, we are less discerning and more accepting. For example, a fascinating study showed that parole court judges were 65 percent more likely to grant parole right after breakfast or lunch than at other times (in fact, at the furthest point from a meal break the rate of favorable parole decisions fell to zero).[9]

- Sit the person you want to influence in a comfortable chair. The comfort can induce a feeling of wellbeing and safety not dissimilar to that which we feel after eating a meal. Make sure that the chair is not so deep that they cannot get out of it quickly as this can induce a sense of panic. Genetically, we are wired to need the feeling that we can instantly spring into action (to avoid the cheetah on the savannah). Many chairs, particularly in reception areas, are too deep or too low to the ground to give the sitter a true sense of safety. Genetically, we are more predisposed to make a favorable decision if we feel safe and comfortable. If we feel we cannot get out of the chair quickly, we will feel trapped and the resulting anxiety will render us much less open to persuasion.[10]

- Avoid noisy surroundings. Excessive noise tends to activate stress hormones such as cortisol and noradrenaline which in turn will block persuasion. Also, noisy surroundings force you and the target to sit too close to each other with the danger that you will, inadvertently, violate their defensible space.

- Take up space in the chair – make yourself look imposing. Like many other mammals, humans tend to be impressed by size. This is one reason why men get promoted to the top more than women – they can have a more "commanding" presence. Obesity is not an influencer, but the ability to command space is.

- Choose hefty paper when using documents to aid persuasion. People subconsciously equate thick paper with substance, authority, and "gravitas".

- Keep your voice quiet and in a low register. Lower voices are trusted more than higher ones. Studies have shown that men and women with deeper voices tend to be trusted more and are thus more persuasive.[11]

Conclusion

To recap, the 10 commandments of effective persuasion are:

1. Smile often;

2. Praise judiciously, concretely, and often;

3. Never criticize or denigrate someone's beliefs or assumptions – avoid saying "you are wrong";

4. Ask far more than tell;

5. Make statements that imply you would like an ongoing relationship;

6. Stress what you have in common;

7. Choose quiet, comfortable surroundings;

8. Stay relaxed – your anxiety will lead people to doubt you;

9. Show respect for people's needs and boundaries, and make your own needs known; and

10. Offer nourishment – even just a coffee.

References

1. Mullainathan, S. and Shleifer, A., "Persuasion in finance", *National Bureau of Economic Research*, working paper # 11838, 2005.

2. Gellner, E., "Trust, Cohesion, and the Social Order", in Gambetta, D. (ed.), *Trust: Making and Breaking Cooperative Relations*, electronic edition, Department of Sociology, University of Oxford, 2000, pp. 142–157.

3. Sippy, T. et al., "Cell-Type-Specific Sensorimotor Processing in Striatal Projection Neurons during Goal-Directed Behavior", *Neuron* 88:2, 2015, pp. 298–305.

4. Goleman, D., *Emotional Intelligence*, Bantam, New York, 1995.

5. Arck, P. et al, "Is there a 'gut–brain–skin axis'?", *Experimental Dermitology*, 19:5, 2010, pp. 401–405.

6. Grahn, J.A. et al, "The cognitive functions of the caudate nucleus", *Progress in Neurobiology*, 86:3, 2008, pp. 141–55.

7. Rock, D., "SCARF, a brain-based model for collaborating with and influencing others", *Neuroleadership*, 1, 2008, pp. 44–52.

8. Buck, R. et al, "Emotion and reason in persuasion: applying the ARI model and the CASC Scale", *Journal of Business Research*, 57:6, 2004, pp. 647–656.

9. Danzinger, S. et al, "Extraneous factors in judicial decisions", *Proceedings of the National Academy of Sciences*, 108:17, 2011, pp. 6889–6892.

10. Teodorescu, B., "Internal mechanisms of persuasion", *International Letters of Social and Humanistic Science*, 12, 2014, pp. 73–78.

11. Klofstad, C. et al, "Perceptions of Competence, Strength, and Age Influence Voters to Select Leaders with Lower-Pitched Voices", *PLOS One*, 7 August 2015.

Chapter 9:
Driving trust at all levels

In this chapter we will:

- Have a quick look at the science of trust;

- Examine each of the "five Cs" of trust and show how to make them work for you; and

- Give you some ideas of how you can increase the level of trust in your firm.

"As you can see, the scores are dreadful!" This was the opening remark that the COO of a major multinational firm made when we first met him in one of their very prestigious Wall Street meeting rooms. He pushed over the printout of the engagement scores of the firm's support staff. And they were dreadful. "What can you guys do about it?"

When we looked at their engagement survey, it became apparent that trust was low, which did not surprise us. Low engagement scores are almost inevitably associated with low trust scores. The situation is really much worse than that because almost every engagement survey considerably overstates the level of real engagement in an organization.

One thing has stood out in almost all large firms we have surveyed or worked with over the last 20 years: the lack of trust at many levels. Most law leaders assume that they are trusted by the partners in their firm, and by the rest of the employees. In truth, few of them really are. It may seem odd, but part of this is simply how evolution has designed our DNA to operate. To some extent, disengagement and distrust are inevitable in any mid-to-large size organization. We tend to trust those with whom we have the most day-to-day contact, and to be skeptical about the intentions of those we see less often.

On the savannah, we depended totally for our survival on the support of a small (rarely over 100 members) hunter-gatherer band with whom we interacted all day every day. Over millions of years, this trust of smallness became a genetic trait and also part of our neurophysiology – our brains are still unable to maintain genuine relationships with more than 150 individuals.[1]

Yet without trust organizational change, innovation, and flexibility are extremely difficult, if not impossible. Without these attributes, at all levels, any law firm today is in deep trouble. In fact, recent research has shown that, of the 70–90 percent of change initiatives that fail, lack of trust is a major factor in over 90 percent of those failures.[2]

Firms, like countries in which there is a demonstrable lack of trust, are markedly poorer and less profitable than those with a higher level of trust. The correlation seems to be universal. Since we need trust in order to really progress and change, it would be a good idea to know what – according to the latest research – trust actually is and how you can create it in your firm.

There are five key elements in trust – we call them "the five Cs" because they all begin with – surprise, surprise – the letter C:

- Concern for another person;
- Commonality – the things you have in common with another person;
- Communication – face-to-face communication, preferably;
- Consistency; and
- Competence – the perceived ability to keep your promises.

Though individual people place more or less importance on different elements in this list, overall, the first three are easily the most important. If a leader or manager is seen as deficient in any of these five, they will not be trusted by a sizable part of the workforce.

The science of trust

Like puppies, human babies are born wide-eyed and trusting. They will usually smile at anyone; they will reach out for almost anything – a finger, a hand, a toy. Adults respond to the wide eyes and the infectious smile and feel protective. It's all genetic. We generally feel the same way about puppies, calves, and foals – in fact, almost any baby mammal.

Between baby and adult there's a mutuality of trust. This mutuality is important. We don't feel the same protective trust if the baby doesn't smile, if the foal runs away from us, or the puppy ruins our shoe. A baby can withdraw trust if an adult turns away, or doesn't smile. Trust is mutual.[3] We will find it difficult to trust anyone who shows, by their actions, expression, or gestures, that they do not trust us.

Statistically, over 50 percent of law leaders do not trust those who report to them.[4] And yet most of these esteemed men and women expect to be trusted. In fact, they assume that they *are* trusted.[5] Perhaps they also assume it goes with the job. Unfortunately, as a 2007 study by the John F. Kennedy School of Government at Harvard showed, the reverse is true. As in most other substantial organizations, 70 percent of those who work in large law firms don't trust the organization's leadership. The catch is, just as you can't effectively lead people who don't trust you, so you can't expect to effectively lead people if you don't trust them.

In the brain, trust is very much the result of the action of a neuro-chemical, which we've encountered in early chapters, called oxytocin. It's one of the brain's most powerful agents and, besides trust, it is involved in forming and cementing relationships, pain mitigation, childbirth, etc. Every animal that is capable of having relationships has oxytocin receptors in its brain – even crocodiles, fish, bees, and ants. Until recently, we thought that crocs didn't form relationships; now we know better. The female of any species generally has more receptors, but that's another story.

The brain region which is largely responsible for deciding on whether to trust is the amygdala/striatum axis. The amygdala makes a decision as to whether a person or a situation is threatening or non-threatening and, if it decides that there is no threat present, it passes that infor-mation to the striatum, which makes the initial decision to trust or not. This is where the oxytocin comes in. This chemical messenger is responsible for conveying the message to the caudate – one of the relationship decision centers of the brain – as well as to other areas such as the hippocampus (memory) and the ventral prefrontal cortex (reward value assessment).

In the adult system, trust is not automatically given. In fact, it's with-held until certain actions or expressions are forthcoming, and it depends to some extent on the length of time that people have known each other. Trust does not depend on how much you like someone. You can dislike a person and still trust them and, by the same token, like a person you don't trust. As a law leader, you don't have to be liked to be trusted. In fact, there's one British law leader we know who is universally liked and also pretty well universally distrusted. It's a situation he is totally unaware of.

It seems strange, but liking and trusting are both the result of the uptake of oxytocin by the same neural receptors, but are triggered by quite different stimuli. Which is where we come to the five Cs.

The five Cs of trust

In a trusting relationship, the behavior of both parties must conform to some or all of the five Cs mentioned above, which stimulate the brain to uptake oxytocin. I cannot trust you if you don't trust me. Trust can be partial (if some, but not all, of the Cs are demonstrated), it can be conditional (the parties haven't known each other long, but a number of the Cs are already met). Politicians are mostly only conditionally trusted, as is any newly appointed law leader. Often, we place trust in someone who reminds us strongly of someone we have trusted in the past. We "transfer" the trust to them. Leaders can sometimes benefit from this as they can be seen as parental figures. Trust can also be transactional (the parties only trust each other to perform certain tasks).

Trust is also conditional on power. Someone in a more powerful position is able to take more of a risk in placing trust because they are able to more easily enforce a consequence if that trust is broken. This is undoubtedly why more leaders trust their reports than reports trust their leaders. A leader must therefore put more effort into creating trust than a follower – their firm depends on it. However, no matter what kind of trust it is, it will be based on the five Cs.

1. Concern

We are biologically conditioned to trust those who we perceive are taking a risk on our behalf. For example, if a partner takes the time to coach their reports even though they would be personally better off spending the time on billable work, they create trust – not just in the mind of the lawyer they coach, but in others of similar rank to the lawyer who observe the partner's actions. This is due to the action of what are called "mirror cells", which enable us to feel empathy, as well as oxytocin. In a sense, we get a pleasurable feeling from observing concerned behavior and we bond with those showing it.

In the depths of the great financial crash (GFC), many firms began laying off people, even partners. Whenever this happens, the engagement levels of those remaining fall off – not just because they feel sympathy for those let go, but also because of fear for their own survival. Even if they rationalize that it had to happen because of the financial situation, the sense of betrayal is still there. Trust is weakened by the apparent lack of concern. This may be why 60 percent of downsizing initiatives fail to meet their objectives.[6]

During the GFC, a number of firms bucked the trend and strove to protect their workforce, lawyers, and others. For example, Am Law 100 firm Gibson, Dunn & Crutcher, took a risk by announcing that there would be no lay-offs. Like a number of other outfits, they showed concern, and they were rewarded with engagement and trust, and a considerable rise in revenue.

TOP TIP

Often, it's not enough to take a risk for someone. It only creates trust if that person is aware that you're taking a risk for them. Like Gibson Dunn, don't keep it a secret.

2. Commonality

Trust is based on having a sense that the other person is of the same tribe. We used to think that hunter-gatherer bands were largely kin groupings. We even thought that altruism was confined to those who shared genetic similarities – Richard Dawkins' famous and highly influential book *The Selfish Gene* was based on this notion. We now know that this is false, both in terms of genetics and in terms of the structure of hunter-gatherer bands.

For a start, we are able to perform altruistic acts on behalf of those who are not remotely genetically related to us, or even of the same species (or animal charities would have long ago ceased to exist). Secondly, recent research on the genomes of hunter-gatherers shows that their bands were not made up entirely, or even mostly, of near kin.

What draws humans together, what keeps them united is what they share – common values, common language, common assumptions, common behaviors, common beliefs.[7] Over the millennia, evolution has ordained that we have a genetic propensity to trust, and defend, those that we have most in common with.

Often, the other lawyers do not trust the partners because they feel that they are not part of the same tribe. In many firms, there's the same division between the legal and non-legal personnel. Oddly enough, few law firms make any attempt to overcome this.

One large law firm we work with went some way towards breaking down these barriers by creating a "behavioral charter", a set of behaviors to which all members of the firm – partners, lawyers, and non-legal staff – were expected to adhere. What made this work was that all those who worked at the firm got an equal say in what behaviors went into the charter. It was a bottom-up exercise as opposed to the usual top-down implementation of "values" which are often foreign to most of the staff and anyway bereft of concrete behaviors which would make them real. The 10 behaviors that they arrived at are shown in Table 1.

Rank	Behavior
1	We acknowledge peoples' contributions and give praise
2	We tell the truth
3	We work together to achieve common goals
4	We share helpful knowledge, information ,and resources
5	We do what we say we will do
6	We are unfailingly courteous; we say hello, please, and thank you
7	We don't dwell on mistakes but help people learn and improve
8	We admit mistakes
9	We clearly say what we mean and need of each other
10	We are responsible for our actions

Table 1: A law firm's behavioral charter

According to our surveys, the charter process gave employees and partners a strong sense of commonality and increased both trust and engagement.

The brain looks for the number of commonalities, and on the face of it they can be quite trivial. A shared name, birth place, kind of pet, school, make of car, job, support for the same team, liking of the same sport, distaste of the same politician, and so on almost ad infinitum. In fact, some 70 percent of our conversations are gossipy (not of the malicious kind) searches for commonality.

We ran a program for the executives of a major bank not long ago and we explained how the human brain was geared not for "important stuff", but rather to search for that which we have in common with other humans. It is a search for a basis for trust. Are we part of the tribe that are fans of Tom Cruise? Do we both think the invasion of Iraq was wrong? Do we agree that the drought has more to do with climate change than El Nino?

It is reckoned that the brain initially makes up its mind to trust in less than half a second. It does this partly on the basis of immediate commonalities detected by the senses – similar clothes, similar age, similar scent, similar accent. If there are sufficient of these, the brain is programmed to search more deeply for others. This is primarily why a good questioning technique is so vital – it is through astute questioning and listening that we discover commonalities with other people that may not be apparent at first glance. This enables us to get beyond some aspects of unconscious bias due to apparent differences.

"I've got it!", the CFO of the bank declared at the end of the program. "It's the gossip we indulge in before the exec-co meeting that matters; not what we say in it." In terms of team building and trust creation, he was certainly right.

TOP TIP

The strongest commonalities are mutually agreed behaviors and rituals.

3. Communication

To a human being, what you communicate is far less important than how and how often you do so. The subject matter of any conversation was described by a prominent researcher as being "the snowball on top of the iceberg".[8] It's the excuse for the dialogue or the interaction, not the reason. The reasons lie much deeper. Humans are about relationships, and emotions connected with relationships, not facts and reasoning. In a sense, every communication is about the same basic questions: Are you, really or potentially, part of my support network or not? Can you meet my needs? Are you part of my tribe? Are you a threat or not?

There are two essential elements of communication, as far as trust goes. These are:

- It should be face to face; and
- It needs to be frequent.

Face-to-face is best

We initially gauge the level of trust to place in someone through all of the senses, not just our ears or eyes. If we can't hear, touch (at least potentially), smell, or see the other person, we don't have enough information for the amygdala to make the judgment to lower its guard and allow trust to happen. This is why so many studies have shown that face-to-face communication tends to elevate trust and most forms of electronic communication reduce it.

For trust to happen, our eyes need to be able to watch the other person's body language, scan for emotional reactions to what we are saying or doing, and examine their eyes (we are really looking at the muscles to the side of the right eye which are a give-away for insincerity) and mouth (particularly a couple of little muscles on each side of the mouth which twitch when you lie) to judge the veracity of what they are saying. Our ears need to be able to listen to changes in voice tone to judge changes in emotional content (Is what they're saying really important to them? Are they making fun of me?). We need to smell the phenomes the other person gives off to sense the level of their fear or anxiety, or even love.[9]

Almost none of this information reaches the conscious mind. In a communication, we don't consciously decide to trust, it happens due to the interplay of brain areas such as the amygdala, the striatum, and the nucleus accumbens (the reward center of the brain) enabled by oxytocin and dopamine (the reward neurochemicals). The thinking part of the brain – the prefrontal cortex – is merely the ratifier of a decision already made.

None of this sensory input can be received via text or email. Even the telephone is limiting in terms of trust. Video conferencing is an improvement, and certainly better than any of the above, but far from perfect. In terms of trust creation, face-to-face is king.

Communication must be frequent

The other important point about communication is that it has to be frequent. A human's greatest fear is of abandonment; we are literally constantly looking to see if we are still accepted or are rejected by those whom we have judged to be part of our support network.

In a hunter-gatherer band, the members are with each other 24/7 and communicate very often. We are genetically wired to need that frequency. If we don't have it we sense, or more accurately we *fear*, something is wrong with the relationship. The only exceptions to this can be those who did not receive secure attachment as children. For many of them, safety is in not having frequency of communication.

Partners often tell us that they don't maintain regular communication with their clients, or potential clients, because they don't want to pester them, or to be seen as a nuisance. Well, it's true that they will be seen that way if they go in with the intention of "selling" their services. The act of selling is part of the snowball on top of the iceberg that humans don't care about. But if they go in with the intention of using the exchange of information to deepen the relationship and to demonstrate support through genuine interest in the client, then they will be welcomed and the firm's services will be hired as a reciprocal gesture to maintain the support.

If, on the other hand, the partner stays away, the client may well feel that they were mistaken in their original favorable judgment and withdraw trust. We hear this often from the other side. Our clients tell us that those lawyers who "can't be bothered maintaining contact" or who "are only interested in us as a source of work" rarely, if ever, get given matters – even when they're the most suitable ones to handle it. Being the best M&A lawyer in the world doesn't guarantee you M&A work.

TOP TIP

Make sure that all your lawyers – partners or others – are trained to make frequent, "unsalesy" face-to-face contact with actual and potential clients.

4. Consistency

In terms of trust, consistency is closely tied in with the human need for certainty, and this need is one of our primary drivers. All mammals are programmed to try to predict what another animal will do in any situation. It's a survival need and humans are no different. We trust more those that we can predict.

The best way to promote trust is to consistently do the right thing, in relationship terms, for other people – to be there for them and to show you care. This garners the most trust because it encourages the nuclear accumbens to increase the dopamine and oxytocin to the appropriate neural receptors in the trust areas of the brain. However, if you find consistently doing the right thing difficult, at least be consistently bad. The predictive quality of your behavior will mitigate against the stress-hormone reaction that your not-so-good actions provoke. The worst thing is to flip-flop between the two.

Some of the real nasties of the last century – Adolph Hitler, Pol Pot, Mao Tse Tung – inspired loyalty and trust in their followers in part because they were very consistent in their (very bad) behavior. However, in the end, it's those who behaved consistently well that have had the greatest impact and have provided the most benefit to their organizations and to society as a whole. Think Mahatma Gandhi, Lee Iacocca, or Bill Gates.

With someone you trust, go over your actions over the last year and see how they rate on the consistency scale.

5. Competence

In terms of trust, competence has a rather limited meaning and that is "the perceived ability to fulfil the promises you make". People trust you to the extent that they believe you will be able to do what you say you will. It is essentially forward-looking. It is what politicians, and aspirant managing partners, use to try to convince their respective electorates that they can be trusted. Of course, if you fail to fulfil your promises you lose some trust – but not entirely. If you've built up a strong relationship with someone – and you are meeting their trust needs in other ways – they will give you any number of second, or third, or fourth chances.

That is why competence is the weakest of the five elements of trust. Yet this is the one which most firms stress when they ask their clients, or potential clients, to trust them. Their partners and other lawyers would do much better consistently getting their communication right, stressing their commonality, and being seen to go out of their way for their clients.

Never make promises that you don't know for sure you can keep.

Making the firm trustworthy at all levels

In a large firm, you will never get perfect trust at all levels. However, you can make any firm more trustworthy internally and externally. In most firms – except the very small – creating trust is a question of examining everything that the firm does, from its cultural norms to its client interactions, to its processes in the light of the five Cs. For example, you might ask:

- How do you communicate? In many firms, communication is predominantly by email or other electronic means. Often, this is because of geographic distance. However, we have often seen partners, and others, send emails to people just a few desks away. This is fine if you're sending a document, or something else that needs to be in writing, but for anything else it is so much better just to get up and go to speak to the other person.

- Are the partners prepared to take a risk for each other, or for their teams? Not usually. There was a quote in one of the leading Australian law magazines by a partner who had moved from a large firm to a much smaller one to the effect: "I left because I found out that my greatest rival was not in another firm, but in the office next to mine."

- Do the partners seem to create separation between themselves and the rest? Yes, although many professional services firms seem to see that this is bad both for business and for staff morale and are taking steps to overcome it. For example, the UK branch of the accountancy firm Grant Thornton (known as "number 5 of the Big 4") is rolling out a program designed to make all those who work there feel genuinely owners of the business and to reduce the disparity, even in income, between the partners and the rest. Unfortunately, in law this does not seem to be happening to any extent.

- Are the firm's leaders engaged in the process of creating commonality not just with the partners, but also with the lawyers, support staff, and clients? No. Commonality is not generally considered, much less considered important.

- How consistent is the behavior of the firm's leaders and partners? In our observation many partners are consistently good, and the majority certainly would like to be. There are, unfortunately, a minority in every large firm who are consistently bad in their behaviors – especially to non-partners – and a large number who flip-flop. One of the big problems is that, in most law firms, bad partner behavior is rarely punished and there is usually no mechanism for rewarding consistently good behavior.

The effects of stress on trust

We believe that the root of many of the problems listed above is the pressure – the stress – that partners and non-partners are under in most law firms. It is this stress which leads so many to be either addicted to alcohol or drugs[10] or to have a really unfortunate home life. The divorce rate among lawyers (especially women lawyers) is higher than that found in other professions.[11]

Addiction to any substance is known to be a trust killer. And it's increasingly recognized that this includes addiction to work.[12] People within the legal profession are generally unaware that working long hours can lead to an addiction to work – "workaholism", as it's called in popular literature. This is another way of saying that the long hours can give the worker a sense of achievement, pride, maybe even importance. Certainly, in today's law firm it can lead to admiration. All these – achievement, pride, sense of importance, and admiration – stimulate the nucleus accumbens to send dopamine to the reward and pleasure areas of the brain and set up a vicious cycle which leads, eventually, to addiction.

Conclusion

Many managing partners and other law leaders we speak to claim that this stress is inevitable and that lawyers have to just "be tough enough to get on with it". We beg to differ. It may not be possible to create a situation of perfect trust in any large organization. But you can go a long way towards creating the conditions in which the five Cs can operate most effectively.

You can reduce stress in simple, inexpensive, ways. For example you can:

- Change your management style to be more transformational, more inclusive;
- Punish egregious behavior;
- Make work more social in nature;
- Praise, and reward, collaboration rather than competition; and

- Even introduce potted plants and paintings or photographs of scenes of nature.

All of these are covered elsewhere in the book. As you decrease stress, you give people a chance to concentrate more on the five Cs. The interesting thing is that as you increase the level of trust within the firm, you increase the trust that clients and potential clients have in the firm.[13]

References

1. Dunbar, R., How Many Friends Does One Person Need?: *Dunbar's Number and Other Evolutionary Quirks*, Faber and Faber, London, 2010.
2. Gill, R., "Change management—or change leadership" *Journal of Change Management* 3:4, 2003, pp. 307–318.
3. Zac, P., "The Neurobiology of Trust", *Scientific American*, 298, 2008, pp. 88–95.
4. Seppala, T. et al, "A Trust-Focused Model of Leaders' Fairness Enactment", *Journal of Personnel Psychology*, 11:1, 2012, pp. 20–30.
5. Galford, R. and Drapeau, S., *The Trusted Leader*, Simon & Schuster, New York, 2003.
6. Gandolphi, F., "Reflecting on Downsizing: What have managers learned?", *SAM Advanced Management Journal*, 73:2, 2008.
7. Lewicki, R.L. and Tomlinson, E., "Trust and Trust Building", *Beyond Intractability*, December 2003.
8. Kellett, P., *Language Arts and Disciplines*, SAGE Publications, Boston, 2006.
9. McClintock, M., "Human Body Scents: Conscious Perceptions and Biological Effects", *Chemical Senses*, 30:1, 2005, pp. 1135–1137.
10. The addiction rate for lawyers is twice that of the general population; see Intervention Strategies, "17 Statistics on Drug Abuse Among Lawyers", 7 January 2014, http://interventionstrategies.com/17-statistics-on-drug-abuse-among-lawyers/.
11. Schiltz, P., "On Being a Happy, Healthy, and Ethical Member of an Unhappy, Unhealthy, and Unethical Profession", *Vanderbilt Law Review*, May 1999.
12. Porter, G., "Can you trust a workaholic? How work addiction erodes trust throughout the organization." *Journal of Contemporary Business Issues*, 6:2, 1998, pp. 48–57.
13. Di Luzio, G., "A Sociological Concept of Client Trust", Current Sociology 54:4, 2006, pp. 549–564.

Chapter 10:
Dialogue – The generator of success

In this chapter we look at:

- The potential impact of every interaction;

- The hidden meaning in every conversation;

- Strengthening the relationship to achieve the outcome;

- Identifying mutual needs;

- Asking and listening;

- Praise, the strongest reward and motivator; and

- Bringing it all together in a conversation.

Ironically, as the law firm of the future turns more strongly to digitization and electronic communication, it will rely more than ever on clear, effective dialogue to unite and empower the crucial people who have not been replaced by machines. Relationships run on communication, and the quality of dialogue determines success at all areas of the business of law: winning people over to your views and to you as a provider, generating new ideas and strategy, negotiating and resolving conflict, building trust and confidence, and growing the competence and capability of your people.

Shaping the firm through dialogue

When we think of dialogue, we mostly think of conversation and imagine it as a cerebral (or cognitive) and sometimes emotional exchange. However, the new human science shows the process of interaction to be far more profound. As Daniel Goleman first observed, in every significant encounter we not only profoundly affect each other, we in some ongoing sense co-create each other.[1]

Our words and gestures impact our neurochemistry and even the function of our genes. For example, if your boss or an important client criticizes you, the amygdala will signal danger and trigger the fight or flight stress neurochemicals, noradrenalin and cortisol. This will, to a greater or lesser degree, create a physiological stress reaction such as increased heartbeat and breath rate, flushing or turning pale, perhaps even shutting down of the digestive system. If such negative interactions occur repeatedly, cortisol will hamper the immune system function and make you vulnerable to illness.

At the time, these reactions can be countered by encouraging the parasympathetic system to take over, such as by sitting with a trusted companion and allowing the mirror cell system in each brain in conjunction with the brains' oscillators to communicate with each other without a word being spoken.[2] Studies show that even the presence of someone you trust will stimulate the brain's striatum, or trust center, and the release of the bonding neurochemical oxytocin.[3]

Receiving (or even giving) praise also has a powerfully positive and ongoing effect. Praise stimulates the nucleus accumbens in the limbic system to produce the feel good neurochemicals dopamine (more on that later) and serotonin, which has a calming influence. These neurochemicals encourage the immune system and sustainability. What's more, they open the brain to better function, new ideas, and learning.[4] Rather essential for the agile, entrepreneurial, and hardy firms we require for the future, no?

We now know that the neurochemistry of our interactions is only half the story. The other half is even more profound and longer lasting: the impact on our very DNA. Obviously, how you speak to someone won't change the color of their eyes, their height, or their natural prowess at tennis – these are determined by what are called "hard", or fixed, genes. However, the "soft" genes that govern many character traits such as optimism, the drive to leadership (see Chapter 13), and susceptibility to certain illnesses such as cancer and heart disease, can be switched on or off by experience – and the most powerful experience for a human being is reacting with another person.

Written words without visuals, from email to texts, also have a strong impact. They are far more likely to trigger anger and, according to research, distrust. This is because there are no accompanying signals to clarify the message, such as a smile or tone of voice. Research has shown we rely on unconscious cues to tell if someone is telling the truth. One example is the rapid twitching – far too fast for the eye to see, at 400 milliseconds – of tiny muscles above the mouth when people lie. This is one reason why most of our attention during a conversation is not on the others' eyes, as we assume, but on their mouth.

If you must communicate electronically, be sure to do so face to face. The technology is abundant, and it's surprising how little use many firms make of it.

A firm, just like a family, is literally shaped by the quality of its interactions. And its success is largely determined by its ability to bring clients and stakeholders into its vortex, gain their commitment at the neurochemical level, and even in many cases positively impact the function of their DNA. And the art of doing this well is good dialogue.

Language as grooming

When your cat rubs against your ankles and purrs at her breakfast time, or your dog wags his tail and levitates when you get home, you are probably aware of what they are communicating. At a deeper level, they like the boss who praises you are manipulating your neurochemistry, releasing bonding and other feel-good neurochemicals. These simple interactions have been shown to produce health benefits to you ranging from lowered heart rate to longer life span, even among very sick people.[5]

Before humans had spoken language, we communicated through gestures, basic sounds, and expressions. These probably sufficed for everything except complex group actions such as building boats and large communal dwellings, which came later. After all, hunting packs such as wild dogs are extraordinarily coordinated and efficient. Certainly, science has shown us that logic and facts as conveyed by words are the very least important aspects of persuasion and decision making.

Evolutionary psychologists suggest that more complex human language evolved from social actions such as grooming.[6] In other primates, these still play an essential role in group cohesion and avoiding conflict. Humans retain vestiges of grooming in soothing gestures such as pats on the back or touches on the arm. Raw sounds, from purring to screeching and growling, were also obvious precursors to language.

Nowadays, however, certainly in the business context, we tend to convey these emotional messages and their physiological impact through words and tone of voice as well as sounds such as laughter and wordless exclamations.

The hidden meaning in every conversation

As we have seen so far, conversations and in fact any form of communication has a far deeper meaning and impact than we are often aware of. So, is there a way of breaking down what we're really talking about, or the subtexts of any conversation?

To answer this question, we and our team analyzed where the brain's attention is in any conversation. It's amazing what you can now see through fMRI (functional magnetic resonating imager) imaging of the brain in real-time interactions. Through various techniques such as spotting blood flow, researchers can pinpoint what parts of the brain are being activated, and link these to emotional states and functions. For example, we know that beliefs and assumptions are located in the orbitofrontal cortex, while relationships are largely handled in the limbic system and reasoning is principally the province of the prefrontal cortex. All three are involved in the process of decision making and justifying decisions to a greater or lesser extent.

After surveying a large number of studies regarding brain function during any interaction between human beings and any other sentient creature (other humans, pets etc.), we created a model of where peoples' attention is likely to be in almost any conversation. As you can see in the "Dialogue Subtexts" iceberg model in Figure 1, only 1 percent of the iceberg is above the waterline and readily visible. The rest is in either somewhat murky water and takes some concentration to see (the 20 percent), or at an even lower level (the 79 percent), which requires a deeper dive to uncover.

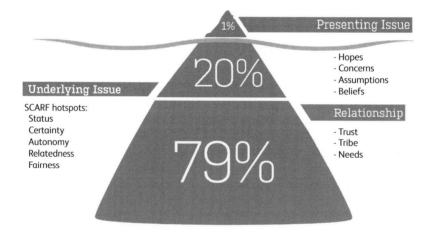

Figure 1: Dialogue subtexts, ©Fortinberry Murray, 2016

The tip of the iceberg represents about 1 percent of the brain's focus, which is on what people think they are talking about – the topic or, as doctors and psychologists like to call it, the "presenting issue". This is the only part we are usually conscious of, such as the details of a matter, your salary, or even which family member is going to load the dishwasher tonight. This is the "what" of the conversation, and the brain is not fundamentally interested.

What does literally "light up" the brain – or 20 percent of it – on an fMRI scan, is the underlying issue or issues. This is why the topic matters. What does the business deal, or the salary, or who does the household chores, really mean to us? How do these things affect our sense of personal value, our hopes, fears, or concerns? How do they reflect our assumptions and beliefs?

The five main motivators (the 20 percent)

A handy way of identifying underlying issues or concerns comes from David Rock's identification of five brain motivators or "hot spots". These have the acronym SCARF, which stands for status, certainty, autonomy, relatedness, and fairness.[7] (A case study describing how one firm successfully used SCARF to *persuade* partners to accept a change in responsibilities is described in Chapter 8.)

- **Status** is about feeling valued in the community or organization. A discussion about salary and a parking spot in the building garage may really be rooted in how valued and therefore safe in their position the person feels. Our sense of status comes not necessarily from a formal position such as managing partner or CEO, but from how we perceive others perceive us.

- **Autonomy**, or a sense of control over our lives, is vital for employee engagement and even optimism and resilience. The more choices you can give someone, whether it is in how they achieve the goals you and they agree or where and when they work, the more productive they will probably be. You can even give autonomy within a conversation by, for example, letting them set the topic. At that meeting, you might ask if they would be willing to discuss a possibly difficult issue such as how they plan to change their behavior to address negative feedback (they will of course rarely say no, but it does give them a sense of control).

- **Certainty**. People crave certainty, as evidenced by their difficulty in accepting change (See Chapter 13). The most important certainty to a human being lies in their ability to rely on their network of supportive relationships.

- **Relatedness,** as an underlying issue, refers to the relationship between the participants and others, not the people holding the conversation. How will the person's salary negotiations affect their relationship with their family, perhaps in enabling exotic holidays to try to compensate for the lack of time together due to work demands? How will the outcome of the matter, or how developments about it are communicated, affect the general counsel's relationship with the CEO or the board?

- **Fairness** is a primal need for human beings. Not only do we get upset if we feel we are not being equitably treated, we also feel discomfort and even outrage on the part of others whom we consider part of our support network or tribe.

Success in an important dialogue will largely depend on your ability to uncover what lies in that 20 percent. SCARF is just a set of headings for hopes and concerns, and these will mean different things to different people. How much autonomy does someone want, and in what areas? What would be a meaningful symbol of status for them? Which outside relationships are most important to them, and what opportunities or pressures do they represent? In relation to the topic under discussion, or even recent events in an organization, what would fairness mean to them?

People's beliefs and assumptions play a highly significant role in any interaction because they act as a lens that shapes – and often distorts – all experience, and of course everything we hear or see. As mentioned often in this book, about 80 percent of assumptions will be wrong, and 90 percent of our beliefs about others will be wrong in some way. Our beliefs and assumptions play a significant role in any conversation, and what people say – even their choice of specific words – will convey vital clues to these assumptions and beliefs.

Needs-based relationships (the 79 percent)

The foundation of any interaction, which represents a whopping 79 percent of the brain's focus, is the relationship between the two or more people involved. Remember that we said that about 80 percent of all of our neurobiology and genetics is about building and maintaining supportive relationships; and that the brain, our DNA, and our experience perform a continual dance. No wonder the immediate relationship, which represents safety, takes up so much of the brain's attention.

Which brings us to two other basic questions: What is the brain actually focusing on in that 79 percent? And what, in fact, is a relationship?

First of all, the brain is on alert for any danger the relationship might pose. It also constantly checks on the status and security of the relationship itself. So some part of us is always asking: "Are you a member of my tribe?", "What do we have in common (which goes to that point)?", and "Can I trust you?". This is true regardless of the length or solidity of the relationship.

It seems to us that a relationship can be defined as the mutual satisfaction of need. These needs may be transitory – perhaps, involving a one-off transaction in which a customer pays for a product – or deeper and long-term, such as being able to rely on each other to tell the truth or point out what we do well.

These needs can also act as boundaries, such as "When I tell you something in confidence, don't tell others", or "In order for me to do this additional piece of work, I would need you to pay me more." Once you understand that mutual needs form the building blocks of all relationships, whether with your client, your boss, your life partner, your barrister, or your barista, you can begin to deconstruct and reshape the significant interactions.

It's important in these conversations to remember that our most important needs – beyond those for shelter, food, and sex – are social needs. You might be talking to a client about how they would want you to keep them informed about the progress of a matter and the costs, and of course you are really talking about trust and how you will help them to protect the relationships that are important to them.

When you delegate work to an associate, you are telling them what you would need them to do in order for them to be part of your support network. The more authority you give them, the more trust you are demonstrating. Of course, the clearer you are about the outcome, timing, and deliverables, the more you are enabling them to win or confirm your confidence in them and thus strengthen the relationship. Likewise, the clearer you are about what you want them not to do – such as let deadlines slip by without prior notice or at least an explanation. This is how needs act as boundaries.

We call this "needs-based dialogue"© or NBD. One additional benefit of needs-based dialogue is that it is a non-authoritarian way of giving feedback or directives. It is well suited for any effective environment, but is particularly congruent to more intrinsically "flat" organizations such as law and other professional services firms. The power of expressed needs does not come from authority based solely on a title or position. Nor is it a criticism with the usual implications of blame for past actions.

When you say "I need this", you are simply stating a fact about yourself. You are also offering the person a way to build or strengthen the relationship with you. As a leader or purveyor of services, the need may be for the greater good of your firm. But as the representative and in some way the embodiment of that firm, you need certain things in order to fulfil your role, and the agreement is between two or more human beings. That's certainly the way the brain sees it; humans aren't geared to have a relationship with an abstract entity. Of course, they can form "relationships" with inanimate things such as cars; the relationship with the car will last as long as the car meets their needs.

Unlike an automobile, the other person in a relationship can always negotiate and counter with needs of their own to enable them to take the requested action. Moreover, they can refuse, or agree and then not follow up, which is often a trust-breaker. The refusal or inability to meet reasonable, specific needs will carry consequences for the relationship, whether they are stated or not. Since needs are the building blocks of a relationship, if a number of needs – or any vital need – are overlooked, there will be no real relationship. Sometimes, this in itself is an important understanding.

As we explain in Chapter 3, the leader or any lawyer who does not clearly express needs – and the consequences if important ones are not met – will never gain the full confidence and trust of colleagues, reports, or clients. They have no functional boundaries, which means they can only operate through some degree of manipulation, unspoken threat, and withdrawal. This can be damaging to a firm.

Working the 99 percent to resolve the 1 percent

So, how do you use the iceberg model to achieve positive outcomes? In any important conversation, the goal is to build or reconfirm the relationship, which buys you the trust to surface underlying issues. With a better understanding of the other person's real hopes and concerns, you can then clarify and usually deepen the relationship by negotiating the needs that might resolve or address the issues. In terms of the diagram, you move from the base to the top: confirm the base of the iceberg, the 79 percent, in order to address the 20 percent and solve the 1 percent. Of course, there will be a lot of iterations as you move between the sections, hopefully deepening understanding and agreement as you go.[9]

The trick is not to get caught up in the 1 percent, as most conversations and meetings do. Since the brain is not really interested in the particulars of the matter or who will load the dishwasher, people get nowhere. They may passionately dispute the topic, but that won't resolve it. Instead, they solidify their position, which really symbolizes something else, as they lay down more and more neural connections around their original point of view.

This starting point is usually based on their assumptions and beliefs, which simply become more ingrained. Hence, the arguments that escalate and what we call "circular debate", in which each person simply lays down more and more information and arguments to support their own point of view. The results are bad decisions, no new decisions or innovation, and often broken relationships.

For example, say the 1 percent (or presenting issue) is whether a client is going to buy your services. The more you understand their underlying issues and what they want, and demonstrate that, the more they are likely to open up about what they are concerned about and hoping for. You can then help them to express what they would really need in terms of more specific and effective actions you might take on their behalf and how you would work together. And, of course, what you would need in return. At this point, you are both working together to resolve the 1 percent, and all that may be left is to formalize the instructions.[10]

Or take a disagreement with a colleague. Until you really understand what the issue means to them (and to you) in terms of hopes, fears, assumptions, and beliefs, you cannot find a way of addressing the problem or know what you are really asking of each other. There can be no genuine negotiation without a clear understanding of each other's real concerns and needs, and how will you know if they are being met? Once you agree on what each person can and will do going forward – and carry that out – the 1 percent will almost certainly be resolved and the relationship strengthened.

Skillfully using the Dialogue Subtexts model© well prevents misunderstanding and creates far more productive and positive interactions. Usually, the presenting issue is resolved, but even if it is not, the relationship is often strengthened, or at worst it is not damaged. We estimate that this process works about 85 percent of the time. Lack of success is usually because one or more of the parties cannot find anything in common (which is very rare), or trust has been irrevocably broken. Sometimes, one of the people simply is not capable at that time of participating in a relationship, often because they are in the midst of an episode of mood disorder or they suffer from certain types of personality disorders.

Asking and listening

Obviously, showing a genuine interest in someone and digging under-neath the surface to find out what is really going on for them are both essential to productive conversations. Oddly, for all the training people receive in some law firms on dialogue skills such as asking and listening, we find that few do these well – or, frighteningly often, at all.

It seems to be one of those things everyone assumes they are OK at – after all, it's just talking, right? Like all the other relationship skills, we are not born with them. The desire to have relationships, yes. The how-to, no.

For example, take listening. Research shows that we don't hear 60 percent of what people say. Which means they do not hear most of what we say, either. In fact, most conversations are largely dialogues of the deaf. Why is this? There are three main reasons we don't hear each other.

1. Reloading

One reason is that we are too busy thinking about other things, often what we are going to say next. This is called "reloading", as if we are simply arming ourselves for our next clever riposte. We may keep half an ear cocked, but we are not really all that interested. We're too deter-mined to prove what we know.

In today's extremely high-pressured environment, we are often too concerned with getting to the next thing we have to cross off our to-do list to be present to the other person. We miss them entirely – often making the conversation ineffective or even alienating the other person.[11]

2. Feeling challenged

Another reason we don't listen can be that someone is saying some-thing – or might be – that is not aligned with our assumptions and beliefs. Often, we feel this is a challenge to our worth and identity.[12] Assumptions act as a filter or lens through which we perceive the world. The brain tends to reject information that seems to go against these. This is another reason change is difficult – it is hard to pierce our assump-tions and biases about the world and take in information that challenges that. So, sometimes we simply tune that out.

We may hear only what we want to hear, what we assume we will hear, or sadly what we are most afraid of hearing. In lieu of really listening, our mind simply fills in the blanks. Sometimes, we miss what is said because we are stressed or afraid. The more anxious we are, the less likely we are to listen well or hear what is said, even if doing so is critical to our welfare. That's why, if we are going to see the doctor about a possibly serious health condition, it's always best to bring someone else along or to at least take notes we can refer to later.

If our old friend the amygdala senses danger, it will minimize all non-essential functions of the brain to ready it for fight, flight, or freeze. And if the danger is deemed extreme, these will shut down entirely.[13] This is why if you are giving someone a negative message about the outcome of their matter, or about their job performance, the person may not be taking in anything you say. They may be physically present, they may even nod their head and calmly exchange pleasantries, but all this is on automatic.

The real person, or their consciousness, has left the room. Psychologists call extreme cases of this "dissociation", or more colloquially, "black-outs". And that is a very dangerous state for everyone concerned.

We know of one occasion in which a CEO gave an executive member (we'll call her Helen) a negative performance review that he had spent days preparing and a sleepless night rehearsing in his head. A conscientious and well-intentioned man, he desperately wanted to get the conversation right, as she was an important member of his team, and he was relatively new. Helen was based in another state and he didn't know her that well.

During the performance review he ran through his rather lengthy prepared speech, laying out in great depth and specific detail all the things he felt she should do better. He even handed her the five-page list of development points backed up by examples. As he showed her out, they exchanged pleasantries about their families. He felt the conversation had gone fairly well and returned to his office with an enormous sigh of relief. Until a few hours later when a very angry board member phoned to tell him that her good friend Helen had called her in tears accusing him of harassment.

The CEO had not been listening. He hadn't noted the tension in her voice. He hadn't observed her clenched hands, defensively raised shoulders, and pallor. He hadn't asked open-ended questions to encourage her to speak and then paused to allow her to do so. It never occurred to him to ask what she was feeling.

He hadn't checked his assumptions, including that she was fully present after the first five minutes and listening to his carefully phrased comments. It is amazing what people will tell you if you pay attention and give them a chance.

The power of praise

If we could instill one simple skill into a law firm to pack the biggest punch, it would be praise. More research has been done on the impact of this skill than on any other aspect of management. Organizations with a culture of praise are 25 percent more productive, and profitable, than others.[14] And yet, when we ask groups in law firms and law-related conferences who has received praise in the last five working days, only a quarter of people at best raise their hands. Often, particularly in certain countries such as China and France, we are lucky to see even a few tentative hands.

As we have mentioned before, praise releases the powerful reward and motivational neurochemical dopamine. Often called the "happiness" neurochemical, dopamine enables the brain to work better and faster and is in fact essential to its function. It enhances both short- and long-term memory.[15]

The most potent of all performance enhancers, dopamine literally rewards the brain in the strongest possible way for doing what the person is praised for, ensuring that this will happen again. In fact, people don't learn from their mistakes except through automatic nervous system reactions such as pulling your hand off a hot stove.[16] There is simply no mechanism in the brain for *not* doing a certain behavior, and of course the more someone nervously focuses on "not doing" it, the more likely they are to do just that.

Of course, you can get someone to change behavior in the short term through threats. But that won't create real learning and sustainable behavioral change. The way to do that is to catch people doing something right and praise them. Reinforcing and building on peoples' strengths has been shown time and again to be the most effective way of getting them to change.

The other nifty thing about dopamine is that it is an opiate. Taken in pill form or injected, it would be illegal. (No one seems to know if its name has anything to do with "dope".) Dopamine is highly addictive and indeed is often associated with addictive behaviors from alcoholism to gambling and workaholism. This can occur because the brain cannot naturally uptake enough dopamine, or because the person doesn't get enough of the good stuff through praise and in other ways.

We often say, not totally in jest, that by using praise you can not only get people committed to you but literally addicted to you. Talk about a powerful BD and engagement tool! After all, if dopamine is addictive and would be illegal if taken as a substance, and you are the one doling it out... Praise, or showing people that you value them, is essential for people to feel secure in the relationship. Since people only attempt change in the context of relational safety, a culture of praise is vital for innovation and agility. If people try something new and fail, as long as it was within certain clear parameters, they must be praised for some aspect of the attempt – even if just for making it.

If you are going to give a hard message or hold a difficult conversation, start with praise or indicate that you want to have or continue a relationship with the other person. We call these "relationship statements" and they can range from a clear: "I enjoy working with you", to "It's great to see you", or even "I know we often don't see eye to eye, but I would like to see if we can find a way to work together". Without the praise up front, the person may be too anxious to hear what you've said.[17]

This can be followed with very robust feedback without breaking trust, as long as that feedback is specific (so they know what to change and can get praised if they do) and forward-looking.

Frequently asked questions about praise

Surprisingly, people often want to push back about praise when we speak at conferences or trainings. It is as if they were afraid of admitting to themselves – or others – how much they need it. Here are some of the usual questions and our answers.

- "Can you have too much praise?" No, the brain can take any amount.

- "What about insincere praise?" Mostly, the brain gets the dopamine hit anyway. But you can overcome the concern by making your praise specific and showing that you value not just what a person has achieved but how they did so. If you can show that you have paid attention in that way, they will probably get the message that you are interested in them and that you care about the relationship. And, of course, your actions must be congruent.

- "How can I start praising people if I haven't before? I think my secretary might drop dead!" (This in China.) You might warn them beforehand. Say you've taken a course on management and are trying to improve. And, by the way, let them know you would also appreciate being praised when you try new behaviors.

- "If I praise someone and then have to give negative feedback or even a poor performance review later, won't that seem hypocritical or give them the wrong idea?" (And the related, "Won't they get complacent?") No, if you praise them for what you do appreciate they will be much more likely to take on board feedback and try to improve.

- "If I praise one person won't others feel jealous?" In a culture of praise, everyone should get a turn.

- "Everyone has heard that you should preface negative feedback with praise. So, won't praise signal that something bad is coming?" Absolutely, it will – if the only time people receive praise from you is before a hard message. There is a simple solution here…

- "Is praise most powerful in public?" Public praise is terrific, but don't limit it.

- "Won't my boss think I'm sucking up to him?" In our experience and from talking to top leaders, the higher up a person is in terms of title, the less overt praise they get, and they are usually delighted. Besides, they still get the dopamine, which helps them perform better. And if they don't see you often, they will be more likely to remember your name, thanks to its memory enhancing effects.

In a culture of praise, people are encouraged to articulate what they appreciate about each other. Leaders should role model not only giving praise, but accepting it graciously and thereby showing that they value their peoples' opinions. One final comment about praise: the giver, as well as the receiver, gets the dopamine hit. We call that truly win-win.

Conclusion
Good dialogue doesn't get stuck in the "topic" but uncovers the real hopes and concerns it represents. Good questioning and listening surfaces these underlying issues, as well as assumptions and beliefs, so they can be addressed. The foundation of good dialogue is a strong relationship based on trust, commonality, and the mutual satisfaction of needs. And don't forget to be a dopamine dealer.

References
1. Goleman, D., *Social Intelligence*, Bantam, New York, 2007.
2. Penttonen, M. et al, "Natural logarithmic relationship between brain oscillators," *Thalamus and Related Systems*, 2:2, 2003, pp.145–152.
3. Baumgartner, T. et al, "Fool Me Once, Shame on You; Fool Me Twice, Shame on Oxytocin," *Neuron*, 58:4, 2008, pp. 470–471.

4. Wise, R., "Dopamine, learning and motivation," *Nature Reviews: Neuroscience*, Volume 5, 2004, pp. 483–494.
5. Allen, J., and Kellegrew, D., "The Experience of Pet Ownership as a Meaningful Occupation" *Canadian Journal of Occupational Therapy*, 67:4, 2000, pp. 271–278.
6. Dunbar, R., Gossip, *Grooming and the Evolution of Language*, Harvard University Press, Boston, 1998.
7. Rock, D., "SCARF: A brain-based model for collaborating with and influencing others", *NeuroLeadership Journal*, 1.1, 2008, pp. 44–52.
8. Watts, D.J., *Everything is Obvious, Once You Know the Answer: How Common Sense Fails Us*, Crown Business, New York, 2011.
9. For more on this, see Murray, B., "You must mix business and friendship", *Effective Executive*, January, 2011.
10. Giacomantonio, M. et al, "Now you see it, now you don't: Interests, issues, and psychological distance in integrative negotiation", *Journal of Personality and Social Psychology*, 98:5, 2010, pp. 761–774.
11. Gunnlaugson, O., "Shedding Light on the Underlying Forms of Transformative Learning Theory", *Journal of Transformative Education*, 5:2, 2007, pp. 134–151.
12. Goleman, D., "Emotional Mastery," *Leadership Excellence*, 12 June 2011.
13. Goleman, 2011.
14. Robnison, J., "In praise of praising your employees," *Gallup Management Journal*, 9 November 2006.
15. Cools, R. et al, "Inverted-U–Shaped Dopamine Actions on Human Working Memory and Cognitive Control", *Biological Psychiatry*, 69:3, 2011, pp. 113–125.
16. Histed, M. et al, "Learning Substrates in the Primate Prefrontal Cortex and Striatum: Sustained Activity Related to Successful Actions", *Neuron*, 63:2, 2009, pp. 244–253.
17. Goleman, 2011.

Chapter 11:
Effective collaboration and cooperation

This chapter looks at:

● The science of collaboration – why we do or do not do it; and

● How to foster greater collaboration within the firm.

Tom Bender, co-president of Littler Mendleson, puts it bluntly: "It's the firms most willing and able to change that will survive. Sometimes we're going to fail, but we can't be afraid of change."

Successful change in any organization, but particularly in a professional service firm, requires a high degree of cooperation and collaboration at all levels. It is no exaggeration to say that the future of every law firm depends on its ability to foster collaboration within the firm and to cooperate with other firms, public bodies, and enterprises outside its walls. And yet, historically, internal collaboration has been the hardest thing for most law firms to achieve. They simply do not do it well because, by and large, they are not structured for it. In reality, many are structured for internal *competition*.

Most of them do try to make changes; they hire consultants to help them get more collaboration among partners and others – mostly to little or no avail. They know that they have a broken system and yet the lethargy is enormous. The larger firms are like huge oil tankers – it takes a lot of energy to get them started and then it takes a lot of energy to get them to stop. They can hardly turn on a dime to change direction, and they are often controlled by senior partners not far from retirement who see every change as a threat to their status or their income stream. Even younger partners often find it challenging to collaborate on a matter with another partner to achieve a better result for the client.

It needn't be so. Human beings are naturally collaborative, and the new human science can point to ways in which internal and external cooperation and collaboration can be made much easier and more rewarding.

The science of collaboration – Why we do it and why we don't
The genetics of collaboration

Humans are highly social, cooperative animals. That's how we have survived as a species. Alone on the savannah in Neolithic times the survival chances of a human being were pretty low, so natural selection favored those genes which fostered cooperation, sociability, altruism, and collaboration.

But we do not cooperate with everyone. There are two distinct and opposite genetic drives that are constantly battling for supremacy within us. The one is cooperative and the other makes us fearful, suspicious, and uncooperative. Both are highly contextual and subject to experience, both childhood and later. This prior experience has a profound effect upon our readiness to make the social decision to interact collegially with those that we work with. This is why many partners seem totally unwilling to cooperate with their fellows, even when they know and respect them.[1]

Our natural instinct is to cooperate most readily with those whom we see as members of our tribe or, more strictly speaking, members of our band. As we've mentioned, we evolved to live in small units – hunter-gatherer bands – which rarely numbered more than 50 or so. Within this small group, we felt safe enough to collaborate fully. It helped that we lived in a state of true economic equality – no one owned anything so the only real competition was over mates. Everyone shared a common goal: the survival and wellbeing of the band, and everyone contributed. No one feared exclusion except for violating clear rules and taboos. Trust was high.

Commonality drives trust and cooperation

If you dissect the hunter-gatherer band you find something interesting. We used to think of these groups as being united by ties of blood – kinship. However, research over the last few years has shown that this is not at all the case. Rather, these bands were made up of people who shared a number of commonalities, specifically cultural similarities in ritual, taboos, and social organization.[2] So long as we share enough in common with each other we are neurogenetically able to recognize each other as real or potential members of the same band and therefore to collaborate with each other effectively.

As we noted in Chapter 9 in the context of trust, Professor Robin Dunbar of Oxford University has calculated that over 60–70 percent of our conversations with each other are actually gossip (not malicious, but what you might call "chatty"). Gossip, he contends, is in fact the most important part of language because it establishes and strengthens commonality and trust and plays the part that grooming does with chimpanzees, or sex with bonobos.[3] We reestablish our support for sports teams, the parties we vote for, the religion we believe in, the shops we frequent, the movies we like, and the latest hits we both dance to. All of these predispose us to cooperation.

Stranger danger

But we are also genetically wired to fear those who are perceptibly different to us. Sometimes called "stranger danger", it triggers the flight, fight, or freeze fear reaction in our sympathetic nervous system.[4] Studies have shown that this stranger danger and the resulting distrust and actual or latent hostility can be a result of almost any difference important to the individuals concerned – supporters of different teams, people of a different race, members of a different socio-economic class, people in higher or lower positions in a hierarchy, children divided into "A" and "B" teams, believers in different religions, and so on almost to infinity.

This distrust is not always conscious; in fact, we would argue that it rarely is, because our brains are wired in the amygdala (the fear center of the brain) to make an almost instantaneous judgment call on friend/foe, trust/distrust.[5] As has been observed in Rwanda, Bosnia, Syria, the UK, and the US, and so many other places, this latent fear of difference can lie dormant for decades until it is surfaced by some trigger.

Only the establishment of other, more relevant, commonalities will overcome this distrust, and that requires frequent real socializing or working together and lots of gossipy conversations.

Why large law firms have a problem with collaboration

The trouble with law firms, especially large ones, is that their structure and many of their processes go against our genetic make-up. Firstly, any organization of over Dunbar's Number – the famous 150 that is thought to be the maximum number of relationships we can form – is inherently too large for humans to really feel comfortable in. That's why most of us find ourselves "siloed" into smaller groupings, which often guard our own turf. Trying to reorganize and break down these siloes can actually cause yet more angst, distrust, and diminished collaboration.

Then there's the problem of who gets what. The most common remuneration systems historically used by law firms also work against collaboration. They cause what a COO of one of the largest firms in the US described as "a collection of sole practitioners sharing real estate". The "eat what you kill" idea is dying slowly and hard, and many of the bad old ways are still in evidence in even the most progressive firms. We still see arguments over fees earned, refusal to share clients, cross sell, or refer work to more appropriate partners.

Open plan? Activity based workplace? Think again!

Then there is the problem of the layout of the modern office itself. The drive to cut costs, along with the promise of wider cooperation and transparency, has led more and more firms to go into open plan offices and activity based workplaces (ABW). These certainly save space and rental, but new research is showing that they have a bad impact on collaboration. The problem is that activity based workplaces appeal to only one personality type – extroverts. Others may feel uncomfortable and threatened and withdraw from cooperation and collaboration. In fact, desk-sharing and hot-desking are disliked by almost everyone. They are collaboration killers because they pit people against each other for space.[6]

One of the problems is that humans need what is called "defensible space". We need to be able to say that a particular space – our home, or office, our car (especially for a man), our table at a restaurant – is ours. We dislike having that space taken away from us, or being made to share it; we become anxious and often even fearful. We may feel threatened, demeaned, or robbed of our status and therefore more likely to adopt dysfunctional behavior patterns in order to right our own psychological balance.[7]

One of those patterns is a tendency to become socially avoidant. Social avoidance is caused by a lack of oxytocin uptake in various regions of the brain and a resulting over-activation of the amygdala, the fear center.[8]

Virtual and cross-cultural teams

Through amalgamation, alliances, and mergers, the larger law firms have become far more geographically spread, becoming more like multinational corporations. As a result, collaboration now increasingly requires working with people of different cultures, norms, and even legal systems. That poses a number of additional problems, many of which are still problematical for the multinational corporations.

Also, like their multinational corporate counterparts, large law firms are faced with such challenges as the speed of change, market competition, and unpredictability of client needs. Increasingly, teams are created on a project-to-project, or product-to-product basis – often, as Professor Amy Edmondson of Harvard Business School puts it, "on the fly".[9]

It is hard for members of these teams to understand and get to know each other. Communicating at all – not to mention the face-to-face interactions required to build understanding and trust and defuse tension – becomes extremely difficult. It is often impossible to just pick up the phone and clarify an issue or share timely information. Diarizing every phone call between very different time zones becomes a negotiation in which at least one party must lose out on sleep, family time, or both. Stress and the potential for conflict mount.

Stress creates alienation

One final point that has become evident from recent science: the kinds of stressors that are evident in most law firms such as overwork, extreme pressure to achieve financial results, remuneration policies that reduce not only money but status, and constant and poorly managed change make collaboration much less likely. The more stress a person is under, the more insecure they will feel in collaborating or cooperating with others.[10]

Many professions have characteristics that can cause high levels of stress: depression and stress are rampant in medicine; and social workers deal with situations ranging from complex to tragic. But lawyers are particularly susceptible to such problems because of the unique interplay of the legal profession and the lawyer personality. It is the adversarial nature of lawyering that sets it apart from other professions, according to the late Amiram Elwork, former director of the Law-Psychology Graduate Training Program at Widener University and author of *Stress Management for Lawyers*.[11]

"By definition, the adversarial system is conflict-ridden, and conflict creates certain types of emotions like anger, guilt and fear, which cause stress", Elwork wrote. "Emotions have different components to them, including a physical sensation in your body—your heart rate goes up, your pupils dilate—and there is a lot of data to demonstrate that chronic negative emotions are bad for you."

But it's not just the job. Psychologists generally agree that lawyers, particularly those in the larger firms, are wired – often through early parental pressure – to succeed, in such a way that makes them more inclined to suffer the ill effects of stress. Because the majority of lawyers can be characterized as "thinkers" rather than "feelers", Elwork believed they are inherently not as good as they could be at understanding the emotions of others – or themselves. "Lawyers also tend to suppress and repress their physical feelings, from having to go to the bathroom to not paying attention to stomach pains", he wrote. "Many of them think of it as heroic."

That approach is a mistake, he maintained, because it has negative effects on lawyers' physical health,[12] and on their ability to collaborate with one another.

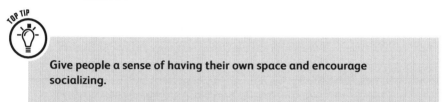

Give people a sense of having their own space and encourage socializing.

How to foster collaboration
Why collaborate?

The first step towards greater collaboration is for the law leader to ask themselves why they need it. Virtually all agree on the need for greater collaboration. It's a mantra that we hear every day from our clients and prospective clients. Sometimes, we ask them why they want to stimulate it. What good does a greater level of partners and others working together actually do? The usual answer is that there will be more cross-selling and greater client value.

Both of these are true. There will be more opportunities to deepen relationships with clients and to provide greater value through expertise. But these are not the only, or perhaps even the main, advantages. Nitin Nohria, the dean of the Harvard Business School, set out the five main reasons for greater collaboration in a well-known paper produced for the 2006 World Economic Forum in Davos. Adapting them slightly for a law firm they are:

1. Cost saving through the transfer of best practices;

2. Better decision making as a result of advice from colleagues – especially those in different practice areas and locations;

3. Increased revenue through the sharing of expertise and services around practice areas and locations;

4. Innovation through the combination and cross-pollination of ideas; and

5. Enhanced capacity for collective action by practice units and locations.[13]

To get these results and to unleash the natural human drive to collaborate, law firms will have to change in a number of ways. They will have to:

- Increase the opportunity for socializing at all levels;

- Make a policy of emphasizing commonality;

- Reduce the collective stress level;

- Increase the sense of safety and tribe within firms; and

- Ensure that all policies and practices reward, not discourage, cooperation.

None of these is easy in today's environment, but all are possible.

Socializing at all levels

Humans will only really cooperate effectively with people that they know well, a point that Professor Dunbar and others have frequently made. And yet socializing is getting less frequent in most law firms. Even before the current set of problems there was little socializing – except a once-a-year party – between people at different levels. There were perhaps partner luncheons and Friday drinks, but the hierarchical nature of the large law firms meant that junior lawyers and others – not to mention support and administration staff – rarely got to meet partners socially.

Effective collaboration is not just between partners, although that is difficult enough. The law firm of the future must be run as a fully collaborative enterprise, especially as the distinction between lawyers and others becomes less and less relevant. As law firms become more like corporates, they rely on the technical, commercial, and increasingly technological expertise of business services such as marketing, business development, knowledge management, and finance.

Also, the ownership structure of firms is bound to change. Non-lawyers can already own law firms in the UK and Australia. The publicly listed firm of Slater and Gordon is a case in point. In the future, there will be an increasing number of non-lawyers in managing partner roles. An example of this was the appointment of business leader and non-lawyer Tony Harrington as chief executive of a major Australian firm, Minter Ellison, in 2014.

Eventually, much of the expertise of lawyers will be in the public domain and freely available to anybody. And a great deal of the work that they now do will be taken over by machines and inexpensively made available by companies that are not law firms. This is, of course, already happening.

In Professor Susskind's view, the very idea of a professional will cease to exist in any meaningful sense. As we point out in Chapter 15, the business of the "law firm" of the future will almost certainly not be law as we know it today. Rather, law will merely be – as Michael Greene, managing partner of Henry Davis York, puts it – "a focus".

So, the idea that partners are somehow special and that they should socially segregate themselves from the rest of the firm becomes less and less tenable. With this realization will come greater mixing, greater opportunities to discover commonalities between lawyers and non-lawyers, and more of an idea that it's OK, and safe, to truly collaborate.

However, there is still the problem of virtual and geographically separate teams. Just as firms are asking for more collaboration and – at the same time – making it harder through growth, globalization, and virtual teams, many are cutting back on travel allotments and socializing in the name of cost-cutting. We believe this to be foolish and short-sighted.

Remember that collaboration and cooperation can only happen if people feel that they are part of the same tribe or band. That can only happen through frequent face-to-face meetings and socializing.[14] Firms seem to believe that video conferencing and other technologies will compensate for the lack of physical contact at less cost. They're right that VC is great – when used in conjunction with face-to-face meetings.

Increasingly, firms have their own in-house videoconferencing systems. One of the major advisory firms we work with has video capability on every phone. Even calling to the kitchen for coffee from a client conference room will bring up the cheerful face of a waiter. The UK-based Stevenson Harwood's Hong Kong office has large screens in each social area that shows the equivalent space on another floor. People wave at each other or go visit when they see someone they want to speak to. Some firms are putting these electronic portals, often wall-sized, in place for offices in different countries. However, it is surprising how underused this new technology is, and it still cannot replace face-to-face socializing.

Make a policy of emphasizing commonality

As we point out in Chapter 7, high-performing teams – or organizations for that matter – are based on a feeling that the members of the team, or the organization, have a lot in common with each other. The same could be said for any individuals, firms, or teams that want to collaborate. They may not feel that commonality at the start of the project, but as they go on this feeling must increase if the project is to succeed.[15]

Commonality can begin anywhere – even with antipathy. If we are united against something we begin to coalesce. That initial cohesion naturally encourages us to explore and discover more positive things that we have in common. We find out that we have goals, expertise, knowledge, skills, and experiences in common. In a short time, we develop rituals, common expressions, language use, and in-jokes. This is true in any culture and across any cultures.

The more we have in common with each other, the more we feel we're a tribe, and the more we will defend that tribe and collaborate so to do.

A firm leader's initial job is to get the members of the firm – all those who work in the firm – to coalesce around their commitment to the relationship with the leader (see Chapter 10). That's a powerful commonality. After that, the leader's job is to stress commonalities shared by all those working in the firm. Of course, a strong firm will be diverse in terms of gender, race, background, capability, and character traits. However, diversity alone does not build trust and cooperation – in fact, it can be a challenge. Genuine diversity can only occur in a culture of inclusion – and that requires people to habitually look for and articulate commonality in order to overcome our innate fear of difference. A culture of looking for what all people do well, praising them, and helping them to build on unique strengths is also essential for both diversity and cooperation.

Reducing stress levels

Stress is one of the main neurogenetic inhibitors to our ability to have good relationships, communication, and cooperation. We have all experienced this at home as well as at work. If we are feeling overwhelmed and anxious, perhaps coupled with lack of sleep or exercise, we tend to be irritable and unable to enjoy – or even pay much attention to – those around us. At work we may become increasingly focused on tasks, place difficult demands on others, or withdraw altogether.

There are many ways in which a law leader can reduce stress in the firm, or practice area, or department that they lead. Most of them are almost, if not entirely, cost-free and will enormously increase the productivity and profitability of the firm, and encourage innovation as well as facilitating collaboration.

Many leaders – in law and elsewhere – believe that it is their people's duty to be tough enough to overcome workplace stress – hence the buzzword "resilience". It is true that some people are genetically wired to cope better with certain stressors than others, but that's not something they can change. And anyway, it's not the point. It's the firm leaders' responsibility to eliminate or minimize stressors, and to help individuals do so, not just their peoples' job to "cope better".

In many countries, including the UK, the US, and Australia, employers have a legal duty to risk assess any hazards in the workplace and take steps to control the impacts. These hazards include psychological stress and there are an increasing number of damages claims resulting from that. There are six main psychological stressors within the law firm environment:

- High demands: Workloads, conflicting priorities, unrealistic deadlines, emotional demands;

- Lack of control: Too little say a partner, or other staff member, has in the way they do their work;

- Lack of support: Too little support and encouragement legal team members and others get from their partner, manager, or colleagues;

- Insecure relationships: This includes the lack of a positive working environment (including a culture of praise), lack of clear, enforceable procedures for managing conflict (especially between partners and others), and unacceptable behavior;

- Lack of role clarity: Practice heads and other leaders failing to ensure lawyers and others understand their roles in matters and projects, and that these roles do not conflict; and

- Bad change management: Leaders failing to manage and communicate organizational change, including adequate and meaningful consultation.[16]

How to reduce each of these is not the province of this chapter, or indeed this book, but each can be mitigated with good leadership and careful reorganization of some of the firm's work or other processes.

> **Ask yourself: What are the stressors in my firm? How can I mitigate them?**

Increasing the level of safety and feeling of "tribe" within firms

Within any modern law firm, the idea that there can be a general, consistent feeling of safety is an illusion. Richard Susskind's widely read books *The End of Lawyers* and *The Future of the Professions* both point to a future which, to most lawyers and law firm leaders, is frankly scary. At the very minimum, there will be a fulsome reorganization of the way lawyers and their firms operate, and at the worst some 90 percent or so of lawyers will be out of work.

At a recent global legal conference Bob spoke at, another presenter discussed the ways that the business of law was going to be taken over by robotics and AI. A managing partner of a mid-sized New Zealand firm asked him what would happen to all the lawyers. His answer was that they should all develop legal apps, sit back, and wait for the money to roll in. Unfortunately, the answer was not facetious.

Yet without a sense of safety, stress reduction and collaboration are not always successful, or even possible.[17] Luckily, there is much law firms can do to create a sense of safety. What human beings want is not just to know that their jobs are safe, especially since they know that no one can guarantee job security any more. But they need to know that the relationships that they have within the firm are safe – that while they work there they are not going to be abandoned, or left without emotional support. If they feel that this is a serious danger, they will withdraw cooperation and collaboration.[18]

A law leader must ensure that, within the firm, it is possible for people to form secure attachments, particularly to the most senior leader and to their group – although this may be at a distance – and to their immediate supervisor. The best way of doing this is to make sure that every leader in the firm is willing to do their utmost to defend and support those that they lead.[19]

In order to cooperate well, people have to understand the reason for the cooperation. Tom Bender puts it this way: "People have to understand the 'why'. They have to be convinced. The worst thing for a leader to do is to just say 'this is what we're doing' without getting out and explaining and articulating the 'why' face to face. They may not always agree with what we're doing, but it's critical that they know why we're doing it."

Taking the time to explain, to convince, and to be seen to take people into the decision-making process gives people the feeling that the leader cares about them and will defend them. People will then collaborate with each other in order to please the leader and to deepen the relationship with them.

Another way a leader can use relational safety to increase collaboration is to make sure that each case of collaboration is recognized and rewarded with praise. The sense of relational safety and status are very closely linked and the more status points that a lawyer or other worker in the firm can get from cooperation, especially when it is not in their immediate interests to do so, the more likely it is that they will be able to overcome their resistance.[20] Of course, all policies and processes must encourage rather than discourage true cooperation and be seen to do so.

Relational safety is the key to increasing the sense of tribe within the firm. Our genetics ensure that once that tribal feeling is imbued people will be more willing to cooperate with each other, to defend the firm, and indeed to change.

TOP TIP

Use the information in Chapter 3 to get greater commitment to you as a leader.

Conclusion

A law leader can increase the level of collaboration within their firm in a number of ways, but it is not a command-and-control exercise. Lawyers, partners, and others will only effectively collaborate with each other if their biological needs – especially those concerned with surrounding themselves with a network of supportive relationships – are met.

A leader at any level of a law firm must take a critical look at all the impediments that exist to collaboration and take steps to minimize them. Major multinational corporations spend a great deal of time and effort doing just that. It is about time law firm leaders followed their example.

References

1. Lee, D. et al, "Neural basis of strategic decision-making", *Trends in Neurosciences*, 39:1, 2016, pp. 40–48.

2. Hill, K. et al, "Co-Residence Patterns in Hunter-Gatherer Societies Show Unique Human Social Structure" *Science*, 331:6022, 2011, pp. 1286–1289.

3. Dunbar, R., *Grooming, Gossip, and the Evolution of Language*, Harvard University Press, Boston, 1998.

4. Coghlin, A., "Stranger danger at the heart of racial bias," *New Scientist*, 206:2756, 2010, page 9.

5. Glaser, J., *Conversational Intelligence: How Great Leaders Build Trust & Get Extraordinary Results*, Bibliomotion, Inc., 2013.

6. Hackson, J., "Personality and the work environment: how well do we fit the modern office?", paper delivered at the annual conference of the Division of Occupational Psychology of the British Psychological Association, Nottingham, 6 January 2016.

7. O'Toole, P., "Observing places: using space and material culture in qualitative research," *Qualitative Research*, 8:5, 2008, pp. 616–634.

8. Kirsch, P. et al, "Oxytocin Modulates Neural Circuitry for Social Cognition and Fear in Humans", *Journal of Neuroscience*, 25:49, 2005, pp. 11489–11493.

9. Edmonson, A., "Teamwork on the Fly", *Harvard Business Review*, April 2012.

10. Liu, Y., "The effects of ego and external stress on group cooperation", dissertation for PhD degree at Georgia Institute of Technology, 2014.

11. Elwork, A., *Stress Management for Lawyers*, Vorkell Group, North Wales, PA, 2007.

12. Pirtle, J., "Stressing yourself sick", *ABA Journal*, 24 September 2006.

13. Hansen, M. and Nohria, N., "How to build collaborative advantage", 2005; monograph produced for the World Economic Forum, Davos, January 2006.

14. Oshri, I. et al, "Global software development: Exploring socialization and face-to-face meetings in distributed strategic projects", *Journal of Strategic Information Systems*, 16:1, 2007, pp. 25–49.

15. Holton, J.A., "Building trust and collaboration in a virtual team", *Team Performance Management*, 7:4, 2001, pp. 36–47.

16. Adapted from Harding, T., "Resilience is not the answer to stress", *Safety Management* (Journal of the British Safety Council), 10 November 2014.

17. Carmeli, A. et al, "Learning behaviors in the workplace: The role of high-quality interpersonal relationships and psychological safety", *Systems Research and Behavioral Science*, 26:1, 2009, pp. 81–98.
18. Barber, N., *Kindness in a Cruel World: the Evolution of Altruism*, Prometheus Books, Amherst NY, 2004.
19. Herold, D. et al, "The effects of transformational and change leadership on employees' commitment to a change: A multilevel study", *Journal of Applied Psychology*, 93:2, 2008, pp. 346–357.
20. Grinde, B., *Evolutionary Happiness*, Darwin Press, Princeton NJ, 2002, Chapter 10.

Chapter 12:
Rewarding people better without paying them more

In this chapter we will be looking at:

- The human neurogenetic reward system;

- Practical lessons learned from science about rewarding people; and

- How to craft a functioning reward system.

Note: This chapter is not about remuneration systems, but about what are called "non-financial rewards" or "social rewards". There's been enough written about monetary rewards already, and too little on the other, more effective and motivating kinds of compensation.

No law firm – or any professional service firm – can continue to pay their people, especially their partners, more and more money. In the new world that we all operate in, there will not be enough there to pay such sums. Even if you get rid of all your non-legal staff and most, if not all, of your junior lawyers, as well as all of your underperforming partners, and even your offices (all of which is already happening), there still will not be enough money.

There are too many expensive lawyers and too few clients willing to pay for them. The day of the £2+ million partner is probably coming to an end. In the end, those highly paid individuals may leave and seek employment elsewhere, retire and sit on a dozen boards or even, heaven forbid, face the fact that their income will have to be reduced. We may even find a new role being carved out for retired partners who have become bored of the boards they are sitting on: partner emeritus – based on the model of retired university professors – where an individual takes space and works for free.

For the firm, any of those scenarios is OK. Research shows that the whole reward system that most major law firms have historically used – offering more money each year – is the most inefficient way of motivating people. It does not work very well over the long, or even medium, term. Why? Because it goes against our DNA. In this chapter, we will show you what *does* work in the long, short, and medium term.

The neurogenic reward system

If a law firm, or any other organization, is going to run efficiently it must have a workable system of reward. Ever since the advent of farming, when we broke with the kind of society that we had evolved to thrive in, humans have been looking for ways to reward and encourage productive behavior. With farming came the idea of private ownership. Reward became the transfer of something of material value from one person or social group to another individual or social group. Modern research has shown that this might have been leading us up a blind alley.

Only over the last 10 years or so have we had the technology to be able to look closely at the neurogenetics of reward – to be able to see in real time what is happening in the brain and to link this up with our biological heritage. And what a lot of fascinating things we have found out. It's causing a revolution in the way we look at how to motivate people, how to manage and lead them, and how to get the best out of them. For example, as a result of neuroimaging studies in 2008 we found out that reputation – and status within a community – was far more important than money in terms of motivation.[1]

A landmark study carried out in 2010 found the neural basis for a much-studied human behavioral trait: altruism. Previous research had shown that we are much more altruistic towards members of our own group (though not necessarily our own kin). The new study also found that those feelings of empathy and altruism towards those in our in-group are great drivers of motivation. In fact, the greatest motivator to action of any kind, they found, is the drive to prevent harm coming to the group we most feel we belong to.[2] This altruistic motivation is deeply embedded in our DNA, and it is something that we share with almost all pack-hunting animals.[3] The finding is not surprising, as many other studies have shown that one of our most powerful drives is to surround ourselves with a nexus of supportive relationships. Obviously, we will strive mightily to protect that group from harm.

What this research shows us is that individual material rewards (money, prizes, bonuses, etc.) are not biologically natural to us and are thus far less effective than social ones. For the first five or so million years of hominid existence (i.e. us and our immediate kin such as australopithicus, homo erectus, homo habilis, Neanderthal, and early homo sapiens), we had no personal possessions of any value. As Oxford Professor Robin Dunbar has shown, we were initially rewarded by grooming, and later – with the development of language and as a short cut for grooming – with praise, recognition, and other verbal relational rewards.[4]

The neural reward system

To understand this better, it is necessary to look a bit more deeply at the brain's reward system, and ask: how does the human organism naturally seek out pleasure and reward? If we can tap into that, then we can fashion rewards that are effective because they are in line with our biological heritage.

Essentially, our inbuilt reward system is there to make sure we get relational support, eat the right things, get the right kind of exercise, avoid things that will cause us pain or make us ill, and encourage us to reproduce our species. Almost every creature that has a brain has a roughly similar setup. In neurogenetic terms we do the right things in order to get a shot of the reward/pleasure neurochemicals, principally dopamine. All the activities that we enjoy, from listening to beautiful music, to eating sweet things, to relating with friends, to making love, we do for a chemical reward.[5]

As we described in Chapter 10, dopamine is the best known and most powerful reward neurochemical. It is sometimes called the "happiness" neurochemical because it directly delivers a sense of pleasure and wellbeing. The promise of dopamine is a motivator of behavior, and the reception of it is a reinforcer of behavior.[6] This is the basis of learning. As researchers initially found with children, threats of punishment in adults are not a successful motivator of good behavior in the long, or even medium, term. One of the reasons for this is that the brain normalizes the punishment or the threat of it and, over time, it ceases to have any effect.[7] This is not to say that the threat of punishment – for example, withdrawal of privileges or, more effectively, relational support – cannot have a powerful short-term effect on individual behavior. Particularly if the threat is to the group to which an individual belongs.[8]

One of the reasons that material rewards are less successful than social ones is that their dopamine effect is short-lived. The brain normalizes the reward and so, as with punishment, the effect wears off relatively quickly. A bonus given this year for exceptional work will be expected next year even if the work is not outstanding. Because of this, partners or others are unlikely to work so hard to get the extra money, and will resent it greatly if it is withheld, inducing them to work even less diligently. This is not so much the case if the financial or other material reward is linked to a social reward – increased status for example.

Dopamine is not the only neurochemical that delivers reward to the action areas of the brain. Oxytocin, the powerful "bonding" neurochemical, is closely related. Since the need to bond is very intense in our species, a reward that delivers oxytocin can be very motivating. The simple act of allowing a well-functioning team to stay together is a prime example.

Another reward chemical, glutamate, which facilitates learning and memory, largely governs behaviors resulting from the reward of food, often the types needed by particular individuals. If you have had experience of training a dog, or even a young child, you know how that works. Glutamate is essential for judgment and self-control. A hungry child, or one who has had too much sugar, for example, will often act inappropriately.

The third major reward neurochemical, serotonin, moderates stress and promotes relaxation. Serotonin plays a big part in rewards such as time off, extra holidays, or the opportunity to relax and take stock.

A deficiency in any of these has been shown to cause various mood disorders and create the danger of a spiral into addiction as a way of making up for the lack.[9] A functional reward must trigger the brain to produce one or other of these chemicals.

It is important to understand that what will work for one person may not work for another since each individual's genetic make-up determines their ability to uptake particular neurochemicals. This affects their response to any kind of reward, and science cannot yet accurately predict that. Also, the genes that regulate the flow of these neurochemicals – the transporter genes – are susceptible to prior experience and present context.

That leaves you with the old-fashioned way of finding out: asking. The only problem with this is that their first response may be one of three really useless but standard answers:

1. What they think you want to hear (e.g. "the work I do is reward enough");

2. What they think is the conventional thing to say (e.g. "more time with my family"); and

3. That they want more money.

Any of these answers might be true, but you have no way of knowing. As the Harvard Business School Dean, Nitin Nohria, points out: "What people say and how they act are, for the majority of humans, quite different."[10] However, if you follow the questioning techniques outlined in Chapter 10, such as asking open-ended questions and fully listening to the answers which you explore further, you will probably get to something approximating the truth.

Practical lessons learned from science about reward

The purpose of any reward system – remuneration, bonuses, social reward – is to change or reinforce behavior. A system of remuneration or other incentive which loses sight of that is, to be honest, pretty useless.

Science has taught us three lessons about rewarding people. We can give them:

- More money. This is effective over the short term, but in the end it simply creates a craving for yet more money without the firm necessarily getting the behavioral quid-pro-quo.
- Social rewards, which are effective, sustainable, and free.
- The opportunity to learn, and the freedom to discover, new things.

Research has shown these to be powerful motivators.

The problem with giving more money

An effective reward system must be sustainable. By that we mean that the effects of the reward must be lasting. Money, or any other material reward, acts rather like alcohol or cocaine. A substantial raise or bonus as a reward for hard work acts on the dopamine/glutamate system rather like a hard drug or stiff drink. The first shot or sniff will produce an immediate pleasurable effect. However, subsequent doses will lead to ever diminishing responses, and to an intense craving long after the pleasure has gone. What's more, the individual's behavior will become more dysfunctional in their attempts to acquire the drug. The desire for increasing amounts of money is exactly the same.

Additionally, these bad behaviors will become embedded in the brain and remain long after the stimulus has gone. We see this in law firms all the time and its results can be witnessed in non-collegial behavior, rudeness, bullying, and the refusal to share information or work.

At a recent law leaders conference, we overheard the following conversation between two of the nation's highest-paid partners. They were comparing the working environment of the firms they worked for:

> **Partner one (female)**: "I am subject to bullying, even by men junior to me. Rudeness and bad language are the norm around the place. I'm expected to work very long hours and I hardly ever get the chance to be with my family. I've even come to dislike many of the clients that I work for. And I've been doing that for nearly two decades."
>
> **Partner two (male)**: "Why don't you just walk out?"
>
> **Partner one**: "I make too much money."

Walking away from money, even if you have no real need for it, can be as difficult as giving up crack cocaine, and for basically the same neurobiological reasons. Like doses of the drug, infusions of money beyond what you absolutely need become less rewarding or motivating; they just become addictive. Money can also come to represent safety and, for many, there can never be enough.

There is a strong argument to be made that the reward systems of many law firms have been a factor in some of their demise. For example, most observers believe that the strongly financial incentive-based system of the Canadian firm Heenan Blaikie LLP was a major cause of its collapse in 2014, and the same is certainly true of the failure of the large, and previously highly respected New York firm of Dewey & LeBoeuf in 2012.

In both of these instances, former partners have pointed to the firms' underlying cultural problems, but most recent research shows that the cultural problems stem largely (though certainly not wholly) from their remuneration systems.[11]

Social rewards last longer

Our neurogenetic system is largely geared towards creating and maintaining supportive relationships. Science has shown that, because of this, the most powerful reward of all is the opportunity for intact teams to stay together. Since humans are pack animals it is hardly surprising that rewarding the group that has been working (or "hunting") together should be highly effective. What a human strives for above all is the survival and enrichment of the group to which they feel most closely attached.[12]

Social rewards are ones that indicate that an individual or a group is supported – praise, acknowledgement, increased status, friendship, group inclusion, group sustainability, and success, etc. These are far more powerful in creating and reinforcing sustained productive effort and behavioral change than material or financial rewards.

It is not surprising that, according to the most recent research, three of the four main reasons people come to work are social. They are to:

- Relate to other humans in a sort of tribe;
- Defend;
- Acquire the means to support those outside the work tribe or to acquire status within it; and
- Learn.[13]

Defending will initially mean protecting a non-work tribe (family, religious affiliation, sports team, etc.), but as they develop close relationships within the firm, individuals will defend those close relationships. It is one of the prime facets of a high-performing team that they will bond tightly together and defend each other.[14] Rather like the musketeers: "One for all and all for one!"

Each of these concepts can be useful in crafting individual rewards and reward systems. The drive for social status is embedded in our genes,[15] which makes it a powerful motivator. The hunter-gatherer tribe tended to protect those of higher status, who also had the best shot at choosing the most desirable mates and the best food. Their offspring were more likely to survive.[16]

The sense of increasing one's status can be gained by receiving public recognition or praise, or by being given more authority – or, of course, through getting more money than others. It's important to remember that status is not necessarily a question of formal rank within the firm. A rainmaker can have more status than the managing partner, just as a shop steward on the factory floor can have superior status in the eyes of factory workers to their supervisor. Status is conferred by the fact that people look up to a person, admire them, or seek to emulate their behavior. Praise given to a lawyer by someone that they see as status-rich will mean more and convey more of a sense of received status than that given by a partner for whom they have no particular regard. In fact, as we have seen in Chapter 10, praise is one of the most powerful of all rewards (and a strong stimulant of dopamine).

The chance to learn something new is also a potent reward and motivator. The brain is a learning machine which, throughout life, seeks out opportunities to learn new things. Henry Ford made the classic remark that old age is when the brain stops learning, whether that is at 20 or 80, and there is a lot of evidence associating an increased danger of dementia with the point when the brain ceases to learn new things.[17] In fact, recent research has indicated a strong causal link between ceasing to do and think new things and our genes preparing the system for death. The immune system is lowered and this opens us up to potentially fatal mental and physical illness.[18]

We give the brain the opportunity to learn by presenting it with new challenges and opportunities to think and reason in different ways. People in middle age and older only get set in their ways because they have not allowed themselves, or have not been given the opportunity, to continue to explore and discover. When people say their work is "interesting" what they usually mean is that it involves new learning and challenges.

But even learning is, ideally, a social activity. We learn best in the company of others because being part of a group actually makes the brain function better – even if we are not directly interacting with other members of the group.[19] So, the reward of being able to learn and discover with others is much more powerful.

TOP TIP

If all your rewards are financial, you are putting your firm in danger and missing out on some easy wins.

Crafting a functional social reward system

There's probably no perfect reward system, just as there is no perfect remuneration system. And perhaps we should not be looking for one. Humans are complex animals with individually differing DNA and experiences and firms exist in a different cultural and business environment. Perhaps all we can do is look for what is functional, what works in terms of the human system.

Some of us will be so caught up in the desire for status, and the material display of status – the luxury car, the palatial house, the expensive school, the $5,000 shower curtains, the upgrade to something more than first class – that only money will satisfy their drive. A managing partner will have to decide whether to make the sacrifices needed to keep these people, or to let them go. If these people are less driven by more social rewards, their behavior may be non-cooperative with colleagues and non-supportive of teams; their effect on the firm overall can be quite negative.

For the others, it's a question of looking deeply at their individual preferences, their personal drivers, the things that motivate them and which give them satisfaction over the long term. Bob once asked a coachee of his, a highly-paid litigation partner in a major multinational firm, whether, if everybody in the world was paid the same, he would still do what he did and work as hard as he did.

"Yes", he replied without hesitation. "I enjoy what I do. I enjoy solving people's problems and keeping them out of legal trouble. Most of all I enjoy working with my team." Bob also asked the CEO of one of the top Australian insurance companies the same question and got the same basic answer. And the same was true of the butcher in the neighbor-hood butcher shop who enjoyed interacting with his customers. His "team" consisted of himself and an apprentice. Professors emeritus sit in universities writing, teaching, and researching without pay. People work voluntarily and enthusiastically for all sorts of organizations, businesses, and charities. In each case, the individuals are getting a social reward.

If someone is not enjoying their work, giving them more money will not make them enjoy it more, or work harder or smarter. People look for happiness and fulfillment in their work. If you can craft their work so that it fulfills their need to relate, learn, and explore and you fashion their rewards accordingly, they will in turn reward the firm many times over.[20]

In pre-farming days, rewards were immediate, obvious, individually targeted, and almost always social in nature.[21] The best way to reward a young child, or a dog, is to catch it doing something right and give it an immediate incentive to continue doing what you approve of. Motivating adults is really no different.

For a law leader, implementing a social reward system takes more careful planning than relying on the standard remuneration system. For one thing, you have to be very specific and concrete about the behaviors you want to reward so that people are very clear what you want. For example, if you want greater collegiality, you must be clear in your own mind what behaviors constitute "collegiality". When you witness these being practiced, you deliver the appropriate social reward immediately (if praise), or shortly thereafter (e.g. through public recognition).

In any case, a more social reward system must be seen to be fair and enticing. But a more social system may mean getting rid of some of law firms' cherished ideas. For example, it means dispensing with the once-a-year grading and assessing of partners and others and rewarding them on the basis of that in favor of a more constant feedback arrangement with rewards targeted to people's more immediate needs and performance (however that is defined). A good current example of this is flexible working in which people can work fewer hours for less of other rewards, such as status.

It will certainly mean getting to know people a lot better, by being more skilled at asking and listening. It will mean being aware of your own boundaries – knowing what rewards you are not prepared to give is just as important as listening to find out what your people want. It will require greater honesty and trust than has been apparent in many of the firms that we have observed.

Some rewards – skilled praise and acknowledgement and developmental feedback, for example – will have to be embedded in the culture of the organization. This will take training since most law firms lack the capability. It will also take time and there will be a lot of people, even senior partners, who will say that this is "all soft and fluffy stuff" – until they see the results in terms of greater enthusiasm among their teams and more loyalty on the part of clients. This will translate into greater revenue and thus more job security for one and all. Law leaders themselves will have to learn to accept these rewards – and their interdependence on others – as well as give them. For some, this will be the greatest challenge of all.

Science, and our own observation over 20 years, shows that a system of immediate social rewards works more effectively on the brain's neural reward networks, and is thus more motivating than the annual allocation of money.

Ask yourself: What other rewards, besides money, can I introduce into the firm and how can I embed them in the culture?

Conclusion

Most firms have realized that they have to change many of the ways they work, and many have also looked at their remuneration systems.

However, that is where it has stopped. We encourage law leaders to look more deeply into their whole system of reward so that financial remuneration is only part of the story, not the whole of it.

Science shows us that money, and material reward generally above a certain amount needed to maintain a comfortable life-style, is not the strongest motivator and quickly becomes normalized. If the only value and differentiator of an employer is salary, then the employer's benefits are a commodity. Moreover, as law firms have seen, once their services are commoditized and the only differentiator is cost, they are in a race to the bottom and don't hold onto clients. The same is true of their people. Therefore, it makes sense to look at the other, non-material, rewards which we know do motivate human beings and change or reinforce behavior.

These are the so-called relational or social rewards. They are powerful because they are in line with our DNA, relatively easy to introduce, and almost cost-free. What is more, firms that employ social rewards will find that they will encourage their people to engage in the firm tribe, bound by deep individual loyalties and the fierce need to defend. Really, it's a no-brainer.

References

1. Izuma, K. et al, "Processing of Social and Monetary Rewards in the Human Striatum", *Neuron* 58:2, 2008, pp. 164–165.
2. Mathur, V. et al, "Neural basis of extraordinary empathy and altruistic motivation", *NeuroImage*, 51:4, 2010, pp. 1468–1475.
3. Boorman, S., *The Genetics of Altruism*, Elsevier, New York, 2012.
4. Dunbar, R., "The Social Brain: Mind, Language and Society in Evolutionary Perspective", *Annual Review of Anthropology*, vol. 32, 2003, pp 163-181.
5. Yegar, L.M. et al, "The ins and outs of the striatum: Role in drug addiction," *Neuroscience*, vol. 301, 2015, pp. 529–541.
6. Wise, R., "Dopamine, learning and motivation", *Nature Reviews: Neuroscience*, vol. 5, pp. 483–495, 2004.
7. Potts, G., "Impact of reward and punishment motivation on behavior monitoring as indexed by the error-related negativity", *International Journal of Psychophysiology*, 81:3, 2011, pp. 324–331.
8. Mathur et al, 2010.
9. Kalivas, P. and O'Brien, C., "Drug Addiction as a Pathology of Staged Neuroplasticity", *Neuropsychopharmacology*, vol. 33, 2008, pp. 166–180.
10. Nohria, N., "The Most Underrated Virtues", *Washington Post*, 23 December 2015.

11. Ordonez de Pablos, P., *Knowledge Management for Competitive Advantage During Economic Crisis*, IGI Global, Hershey, PA, 2014.

12. Mathur, V. et al, 2010.

13. Nohria, N., "Employee Motivation: A powerful new model", *Harvard Business Review*, July/August 2008.

14. Murray, B. "What is a High Performing Team and What Does It Do Differently", *Effective Executive*, 15:2, 2012, pp 53–60.

15. Van der Kooij, M. and Sandi, C., "The Genetics of Social Hierarchies", *Current Opinion in Behavioral Sciences*, vol. 2, 2015, pp. 52–57.

16. Stevens, A. and Price, J., *Evolutionary Psychiatry*, 2nd ed., Routledge, London, 2000.

17. Matthews, F. et al, "Epidemiological Pathology of Dementia: Attributable-Risks at Death in the Medical Research Council Cognitive Function and Ageing Study", *PLoS Medicine*, 6:11 (published online), 2009.

18. Budovsky, A. et al, "LongevityMap: a database of human genetic variants associated with longevity", *Trends in Genetics*, 29:10, 2013, pp. 559–560.

19. Garrison, D.R. et al, "The impact of course duration on the development of a community of inquiry", *Interactive Learning Environments*, 19:3, 2011, pp. 231–246.

20. Pizzani, L., "Satisfaction Reaction: What really drives job satisfaction?", *CFA Institute Magazine*, September/October 2014.

21. Grinde, B., *Darwinian Happiness*, Darwin Press, Princeton NJ, 2002.

Chapter 13:
Hiring for the law firm of the future

This chapter will cover:

- The human capability needs of the law firm of the future; and
- How to select for the personality traits your firm needs.

Hiring and promoting the right people in law firms has always been both crucial and difficult. High cost consultancies and psychometric testing have attempted to remove the uncertainty, but their recommendations are often flawed. And as firms try to adapt to, and stay ahead of, the changes in how business is done and the needs of their clients, building the right capability is far harder than it has ever been.

In fact, law leaders and heads of HR tell us that this uncertainty is driving them to hire more temporary legal talent from on-call agencies such as Lawyers on Demand. As the expanding digital world dramatically changes the need for certain kinds of legal expertise, there is a real question of how to select the few lawyers that will still be required.

Law firms of the future will be in a different business than was traditionally their province, and they will require a different sort of person. There are many theories as to what that person will look like. Mostly, the lawyer of the future is seen as a combination of a rain-maker and the handmaiden to IBM's Watson. Richard Susskind, in his latest book *The Future of the Professions*, says that all professionals – including lawyers – will need "to have mastery over massive bodies of data that bear on their disciplines". Maybe, but our own sources and experience plus the findings of the new science – what we call human science – seem to shed doubt on this.

The human capability needs of the law firm of the future

In the final chapter of this book, we will outline what we think the firm of the future will really be selling. What we're positive of is that, over the next 10 years, there will emerge a different kind of firm, adaptive enough to meet a different kind of demand from a different kind of client. That future firm will need people who are agile, emotionally intelligent, very good listeners, able to accept change, challengers of the status quo, and able to think things through creatively and come up with ideas and, more importantly, questions that machines can't. They must also be fearless and relentless in selling their services and ready to do so at a very early stage in their career. Law will be more of an entrepreneurial business than a profession.[1] In all probability, the person who wants to be a black-letter lawyer need not apply.

The lawyer of the future will work in a firm structured differently from the large, or even mid-sized, law firms of today. Nick Grant, director of human resources at K&L Gates Australia, and previously attorney recruiting manager at Perkins Cole LLP, notes that "different practice areas will be resourced using different staffing models. The traditional pyramid model will be replaced with a more flexible structure allowing teams to be scaled up or down as needed."

For sure, there will be fewer lawyers in even the largest firms and there will be less room for graduates and first and second-year lawyers. Clients will no longer pay for the traditional leverage model, so juniors will have to get their experience and training elsewhere.

Traits and skills

There is often misunderstanding around the difference between skills and traits, and so they tend to get lumped together. In fact, they are quite different. A trait is a genetically determined characteristic, while a skill is learned. An obvious example of the difference is in relationships. Humans, as we have said often in this book, are relationship-forming animals. The drive for supportive relationships is a universal human trait; it is built in to all of our DNA. However, the skills that make some people "good" at relationships are learned, mostly by observation in childhood. Some traits, especially those needed in the workplace, are by no means universal and depend on the particular DNA of individuals – intuition is a case in point.

So, what will the lawyer of the future – working in a large or small firm – be like? What are the traits and core skills they will need?

Technological literacy

There will be fierce rivalry for the services of those more experienced solicitors and senior associates who can meet the ever-changing needs of clients. As Grant puts it, these are "Lawyers who complement their legal skills with an understanding of how to leverage technology to create client solutions." However, leveraging technology does not mean that the lawyer of the future will necessarily be a technocrat.

We agree with Susskind that they will have to work with those who have affinity with what he calls "massive bodies of data". However, the future lawyers need not, in our view, be data analysts themselves. In the longer term, we believe that the collection, manipulation, and analysis of that data will all be done by a computer. Issues, of course, will arise; computers can provide solutions, but they cannot as yet take us through their massively complex "thinking process" (or number crunching) so we can judge how they got there and have confidence in their answers.

Relationship and social skills
Many of the new skills and traits that lawyers will need have more to do with emotional intelligence (EI) and social intelligence (SI) than intellect or technological skills. As yet, EI and SI are not, by and large, taught in most law schools.

Mark Rigotti, Global CEO and partner of Herbert Smith Freehills, sums up what the firm will be looking for as "lawyers with a 'plus'". He explains: "For us, the 'plus' could be strong collaboration skills with an ability to connect across practice groups, geographies, and cultures to derive value for the enterprise and not just the person's practice group, region, or local office. This is important for us given the spread of our business.

But the requirements are not static. In fact, it is likely that a whole range of additional skills and traits will be needed over coming years to meet the changing needs of clients, and this may also require different career models to be developed."

As we said above, relationship skills of the kind that Rigotti is talking about are learned. However, because these are tied to childhood experience, not everybody can learn the kind of skills that will be needed. They may have become socially avoidant, or even have developed an anti-social personality disorder of some kind. Avoidance for them becomes somewhat trait-like and very hard to dislodge.

Mental flexibility
According to law professor William Henderson of Indiana University, named 2015's most influential legal educator of the year by *National Jurist* magazine, the lawyer of the future will "have an interest and track record in practical applications, which means they engage in trial and error, continuous general

learning, can acknowledge when they are wrong, and generally can tolerate ambiguity". In other words, they have mental flexibility.

Mental flexibility is an interesting collection of both skills and traits. Being able to readily acknowledge when one is wrong and tolerate ambiguity are inbuilt traits that someone either is or is not born with, though they can be honed by experience.[2] It is similar to someone who is born with the capacity to be a great athlete, but training undoubtedly brings out the ability to win an Olympic gold medal.

On the other hand, the ability to acquire an interest in something new, or to be able to welcome "continuous general learning" is based more on upbringing – one of the reasons that employers of the future must learn more about a potential hiree's past than they have done before.

Language skills

Language skills are going to be at a premium in the larger firms. As they move out of their traditional areas of practice to become, as Michael Greene, managing partner of Henry Davis York puts it, "key advisors with a legal focus" across industries and borders, their partners and lawyers must be able to communicate effectively in a range of languages. A lawyer in Hong Kong, for example, must be fluent in both English and Cantonese or Putonghua. A French partner will have to be fluent both in French and English. Lawyers will increasingly talk to each other across borders in English and to their local clients in the client's language.

The ability to learn a language is a trait we're born with, and obviously where we are born largely dictates which one we most readily learn. As very young children, we can relatively easily acquire fluency in two or more languages. However, this facility declines sharply after 12–14 years old. It is difficult, if not impossible, for most adults to acquire fluency in a new language.[3] The best we can do is to try really hard to learn enough to be understood, and be skilled enough in dialogue techniques and listening to know when we're not.

Intuition

A key differentiator for a lawyer, whether in a large or small firm, or even a solo practitioner, will be in the way that they think. It will be more the way Renaissance Man was supposed to think – to hover above the factual clues and see things in ways that others didn't, to make the intuitive jumps that artificial intelligence can't make, and few people ever do. Sometimes, it's what we call the "blinding flash of the obvious". It's how the best science and innovation take place.

For example, take the invention of Velcro. The Velcro hook and loop was invented in the 1940s by a man named George de Mestral while he was walking his dog in the Jura Mountains in Switzerland. Mr de Mestral, an engineer, examined the tiny hooks of the cockle-burs that were stuck on his pants and in his dog's fur and wondered how they attached themselves. Under a microscope, he observed the hooks of the burs engaging the loops in the fabric of his pants. Burs had been hooking onto people's clothing for thousands of years; de Mestral's genius was to see the obvious application. He took two disparate things – fabric and bur's hooks and came up with something new.

The lawyer of the future will have to have a brain something like de Mestral's because AI and data could tell you a lot about burs and a lot about fabric, but it cannot make the intuitive jump between the two to come up with the "practical application". In many ways, this is the way in which the best lawyers already work.

Scientists have been grappling with the concept of intuition for many years and only recently have we come to a real understanding of how it works. This is largely due to the work of Dr Kirsten Voltz and her team at the Werner Reichardt Centre for Integrative Neuroscience in Germany. Intuition – having really innovative ideas linking disparate things – is an unconscious activity. You can't sit down and decide to be intuitive. Voltz defines intuition as "a non-conscious process exerting influence on behavior by drawing on implicitly acquired knowledge that signals higher processing areas in the conscious brain".[4]

Intuition is orchestrated by the brain's orbitofrontal cortex (OFC), located just behind the ears. The OFC collects information from various areas of the brain's memory system – particularly that system called implicit memory where memories are triggered unconsciously by the brain being presented with something quite different. Some people's brains are just wired to make this cognitively easy, others are not.

Many people claim to be "intuitive", but in most cases this just means that they are linking up with their own unconscious assumptions or preferences, which are also stored in the orbitofrontal cortex. So their intuitive leaps are only to a manifestation of their own unconscious desires or wishes. The trick for the lawyer of the future will be to utilize genuine intuition and avoid being, in the rather more prosaic sense, "intuitive".

In our view, it is the ability to make the unconscious leap to the genuinely new view of problems that clients will, in the future, actually pay for. They won't come to large expensive law firms looking for facts, data, or solutions; those can be obtained from other, much cheaper, sources. Rather, they will be looking for a certain kind of brain and a certain kind of intelligence, backed by experience.

Acceptance of change

Above all, the trait law firms will need is the capacity to operate effectively in an industry where client needs are, as Rigotti puts it, "not static", but constantly shifting. As Janelle Orsi, author of the book *Practicing Law in the Sharing Economy*, told us:

"To help build a new economy, lawyers need to be willing to question everything that has become common practice and convention in the legal profession. We need to be willing to abandon boilerplate and write documents from scratch. We should rethink how we interact with clients, what we do for them, and how much we charge."

Yet this willingness to abandon precedent, or the way things are usually done, is rare, and perhaps particularly so in lawyers who are often temperamentally risk averse. In fact, we know that the overwhelming majority of humans naturally resist new ways of doing things. Change goes through the same neural pathways as physical pain. This universal trait suggests that to our ancient ancestors there was a survival advantage in change resistance. We have, according to researchers, an immune reaction in which change sets off a threat response readying the system for flight, fight, or freeze.

However, just as some people can tolerate physical pain more easily than others, some can more readily tolerate disruption. In early history, although radical change only occurred in response to rare events such as climate change, it *did* occur. What enabled our ancestors to cope with and adapt to these society-changing disruptions? Evolutionary psychologists tell us that people can best accept change if one thing is constant: their nexus of supportive relationships. For our genetic forbears, that nexus was in the hunter-gatherer band, a smaller version of the later "tribe". Today, that vital network of supportive relationships which form the centrifugal force holding our lives together is most often found in two tribes: the workplace and the nuclear family.

We therefore feel extremely threatened by anything that looks like it will disrupt our relationship nexus. In fact, we are genetically geared to protect this above all else. At the first sign of threat, the amygdala sends warning signals to the rest of the neurogenic system, which instantly blocks the new. However, if the sense of relational security in our home and workplace tribes is strong enough, that reaction is countered by the release of the strong bonding neuro-chemical, oxytocin.

Thus, an individual's acceptance of change is closely linked to their sense of job security, their commitment to those that they work with, and their intention to stay with or leave the organization, coupled with the security they have in their relationships outside of work.

This is one more reason that leaders should pay attention to the non-work aspects of their potential hires, and indeed their existing lawyers.

Ask yourself: How stable are the relationships within the firm? What is the level of commitment that people have to each other?

Courage and curiosity

Courage, humor, and curiosity are also traits that the law firm of the future will need in abundance. As Nicola Atkinson, Ashurst's co-head of expertise, sees it: "A truly 'global' firm seeks to provide clients with a seamless and consistent experience and quality of legal service through a virtual network of lawyers and other business professionals. To my mind, this can only be achieved on a robust platform of trust and this demands of our professionals a quite specific kind of mindset: a curiosity about different ways of solving a problem, a familiarity with and acceptance of different cultures and ways of approaching the world, and an ability to enter unknown interpersonal spaces with courage and good humor."

Humans, like the other closely related great apes, are naturally curious. It's a universal trait. However, many have that curiosity smoth-ered in childhood. There might have been secrets in the family that it would be unwise to know too much about and children can become, quite literally, afraid of their own inquisitiveness. Many lawyers, and even partners, may never be able to shake off the burden of this fear or even have the courage to try. Courage itself is a genetic trait which cannot be learned. Again, you either have it or you don't, though a crisis can bring out the trait where it has hitherto been dormant.[5]

The ability to be entrepreneurial

Law firms are going to demand that their partners be more entrepre-neurial in the way that they run their business. Being entrepreneurial is a trait that is partly genetic, and which is then encouraged or not in childhood. For many firms, particularly the small-to-mid-sized ones, "being entrepreneurial" will mean devising ways to appeal to the 75 percent of people and SMEs who, traditionally, have never gone near a lawyer.

Having a lower cost base, independent practitioners and the smaller firms can more readily appeal to this underserved potential clientele. According to Lucy Jewel, professor of law at the University of Tennessee, "the indie lawyer of the future will craft individualized legal products for consumers who wish to reorganize their everyday personal or work lives".[6] Independent and creative thought will be needed to enable people to do more with less, especially as people's work becomes more precarious and the costs of the services that people rely on in order to work – childcare, transport, and so forth – continue to increase and need to be managed. The community-based lawyer of the future may be in a position to fulfill this role.

The future will be, for most people outside of the very rich, a sharing, Uberized economy, with new conflicts and new demands. As the large law firms turn away from the practice of law per se and more towards the role of general advisor to large clients, says Jewell, a whole army of low-cost independent lawyers and small firms will be needed to cope with the new challenges that the sharing economy throws up. As Janelle Orsi, in her book *Practicing Law in the Sharing Economy*, puts it:

"Every community in the United States will soon need sharing economy lawyers, grassroots transactional lawyers, or whatever you may prefer to call these new legal specialists. With around 30,000 incorporated towns and cities in the United States, we will soon need at least 100,000 sharing economy lawyers. And as the sharing economy becomes the predominant economic force in our society, then all trans-actional lawyers in the United States (approximately 500,000) should consider transforming the focus of their practices to smooth the way toward a more sustainable economy. No matter how you do the math, the sharing economy offers a huge opportunity to new and experienced lawyers alike."[7]

Entrepreneurism is not just for the smaller firms, however. A number of the larger firms that we work with have taken the need for entrepreneurialism to heart. Littler Mendelson's "CaseSmart" product is a case in point. It was developed by Scott Forman, one of their partners, and championed by Scott Rechtschaffen, their chief knowledge officer.

"The need to become more innovative and entrepreneurial", Rechschaffen says, "for us came out of challenges presented by our clients. Clients continuously wanted more for less and greater efficiency in delivery of the more routine work. Also, clients increasingly wanted the ability to do things themselves.

We came to see this as an opportunity and six years ago Scott came up with the idea for Littler CaseSmart, a cost-effective and efficient way to handle the defense of equal employment opportunity charges and single-plaintiff employment litigation. We put together a multidiscipli-nary team of 65 people to work on the idea. It was a great success. We later developed 'ComplianceHR', our joint venture with a software company, as a way to tackle another market – people who have moved away from lawyers and rely on Google for legal information on HR matters.

We see the commoditization of law as an opportunity and we are setting out to 'own' it."

Another example comes from a substantial Australian firm where a number of partners got together and, with the slightly reluctant support of the managing partner, went into the business of arranging loan financing from wealthy private individuals who were already clients of the firm, for mid-sized corporate clients who had previously relied on their bankers. This growing business now provides them with an income stream greater than the partners achieved in their traditional law practices. Meanwhile, a number of other professional services firms such as Ashurst (mentioned earlier), Deloitte, and Grant Thornton, are looking to sell the expertise of their support services to other organizations.

As Scott Rechschaffen says, "Lawyers are risk-averse and don't normally innovate", but the examples above show that they can be led to do so. "Some never will", says Rechschaffen. "But those that have the potential can be encouraged to be both innovative and entrepreneurial if they can see it being successful and helping them to win work rather than displacing them."

Selecting for the traits you want

What law firms will be looking for in the future from the lawyers and others they recruit, will be certain personality and psychological traits rather than particular skills, the need for which will be in a state of constant flux.

Testing for the traits you want

According to MIT's Patrick Gunkel, there are 638 primary personality traits of which 234 are what he calls positive (e.g. adaptable, good-natured, resourceful), 112 are neutral (e.g. authoritarian, irreverent, unambitious), and the rest (292) are classified as negative (e.g. abrasive, critical, easily discouraged).[8] Although these can be greatly modified by context or experience, they are all innate to the person.

Though we know that traits are genetic in origin, scientists have, as of writing, no idea of the particular genes, or cluster of genes, that determine most of them. Some we are beginning to get a fair idea of. Aggression, for example, we know to be caused by a cluster of genes, novelty-seeking is most closely linked to one of the dopamine transporter genes, and neuroticism is largely influenced by one of the serotonin transporter genes.[9] The take-away for all this is that we are nowhere near an accurate genetic test for personality traits. A swab won't do it anytime soon!

There are many, many psychometric tests which claim to be able to determine personality traits. They vary greatly in their scientific validity. One of the most widely-used, the famous Meyers-Briggs MBTI, has no scientific basis whatsoever. The rest vary from being more-or-less OK to useless. The main reason for this lack of accuracy is that the genes behind personality differences are what are called "soft" genes that are highly influenced in the way they manifest themselves by individual experience and social and environmental context.[10] So a psychometric test may accurately indicate the overall personality profile of a person at the time and in the social and other circumstances in which they took the test. For example, if they filled it in alone or they were in company, the answers may well be different (as with exam questions). How they felt about themselves that day will affect how they answer. If they'd had an argument with their spouse or the room was overheated, or too cold, or whether the light was from fluorescents etc. have all been shown to profoundly influence the way people answer questions in the tests.[11]

None of these can be fully allowed for when formulating any psychometric questionnaire. Nor can it allow for the fact that one or more of the candidates may be dyslexic (often without their knowing it).

Another problem with psychometric tests is self-deception. People are overly optimistic in their perceptions of their own positive personality and play down their negative aspects. Then there is impression management. Individuals try to appear "nice" because they fear social disapproval.

Moreover, it is very easy to cheat on these tests. A study by the American Psychological Association found that over 80 percent of job applicants actually hired after taking a widely used and respected personality test had intentionally manipulated their answers to make themselves look better. And there are plenty of sites and eBooks out there to help candidates do just that.[12]

The case of Paul Flowers, chairman of the Cooperative Bank, should be a lesson to all those who rely on these tests for recruiting. He was caught buying illegal drugs, including crack cocaine, yet he passed his psychometric test with flying colors. Some of the universities have developed tests which have a fair degree of validity, but even then, experts say, they should never be relied on as the sole source of information about the personality of a potential hire.[13]

TOP TIP

Don't rely on psychometric tests alone, or even too much.

A better way to select people

Rather than seeking to assess personality, the better way forward is to judge candidates by their behaviors. Over time, these will show a pattern indicating the dominance of certain personality traits that would have been formed by the interaction of experience and genetics. This pattern of behaviors from the past to the present can be gleaned by interviews conducted by experienced interviewers over a series of sessions. Their observations can then be verified by having the candidate work in the position for a trial period, or even on a short-term contract and 360-degree interviews (*not* questionnaires) conducted to ascertain their behavior during that time.

Select people who "fit in"

It is also important to remember that a firm is a tribe, and a tribe has certain modes of behavior, rituals, and social rules that govern it and make the people in it feel accepted and valued. It is vital to make sure that the candidate will make a good fit with this culture.

Recently, Bob worked with a mid-sized UK firm that had recruited a lateral partner from one of the Magic Circle firms. In the larger firm, he had been subject to rigid performance targets and regular reviews against these. He had been aggressive and successful. The firm he was being considered for was more relaxed, more cooperative, and less committed to rigid targets. Both firms were very profitable. Bob had an interview with the man and he recommended against hiring him as a partner. He thought that the cultures of the two firms were so very different, and while his past behaviors at school and after showed that he would fit in well with the culture of the larger firm, Bob had his doubts about his fit with the new one.

In the end, the candidate was taken on at the insistence of the managing partner and it proved to be a bad mistake. His aggressive narcissism rubbed everyone at the new firm the wrong way. As Bob had predicted, the man's refusal to cooperate with his fellow partners, his unwillingness to share work, his tendency to talk over people – even clients (all things Bob had predicted), proved too much and he was forced out at considerable financial cost to the firm.

TOP TIP

> **If you want to change the culture of the firm, do so and get the inevitable angst over with before you bring on new people.**

Conclusion

Law in the future will be more of a business than a profession. Lawyers will be business people helping and advising other people in business. They will be in the business of forming solid, "sticky" relationships with clients. Really the only skills that all who work in the law firm of the future will need are relationship-forming skills, in particular being great listeners and skilled questioners.

Most of them will also have to be technologically literate enough not to be afraid of technology, but they must not be wedded to it. Where it helps them to think through a problem, or to better create or sustain relationships, then they must be able to use it effectively. Technology is a tool for humans to use, not a slave driver which dictates every aspect of their lives and work.

Different firms will need different traits in their people (and law leaders must be very clear as to the particular personality traits they are looking for), but there are some that will be universally needed. First and foremost will be the ability to change and to be flexible. As trusted advisors, lawyers will also have to be confident, conscientious, cooperative, creative, and courageous. They will have to be able to challenge existing "truths" and have a mind which is able to think laterally and intuitively.

They will have to be entrepreneurial. It is through these skills and traits that lawyers of the future – and law firms of the future – will be able to truly differentiate themselves.

References

1. Warfield Brown, D., "Self Serving Professionals" in *America's Culture of Professionalism*, 2014 , Chapter 2.

2. Dickenson, D. et al, "Genes, cognition and brain through a COMT lens", *Neuroscience*, 161:1, 2009, pp. 72–87.

3. Abadzi, H., "Does age diminish the ability to learn fluent reading?", *Educational Psychology Review*, 8:4, 1996, pp. 373–395.

4. Voltz, K. and Zander, T., "Primed for Intuition?", *Neuroscience of Decision Making*, vol. 1, 2014, Pages 26–34 .

5. Orsi, J., *Practicing Law in the Sharing Economy*, American Bar Association, Washington DC, 2013.

6. Bouchard, T. Jr., "Genes, environment and personality", *Science*, 264:5166, 1994, pp. 1700–1701.

7. Jewel, L. "The Indie Lawyer of the Future: How New Technology, Cultural Trends, and Market Forces Can Transform the Solo Practice of Law", University of Tennessee Legal Studies Research Paper No. 274, 2015.

8. Patrick Gunkel's list of personality traits is available online at http://ideonomy.mit.edu/essays/traits.html.

9. Azar, B., "Searching for genes that explain our personalities", *Monitor on Psychology*, 33:8, 2002, p. 44.

10. Webster, M. and Ward, A., "Personality and Social Context," *Biological Reviews*, 86:4, 2011, pp. 759–773.

11. Albery, I. et al, *Complete Psychology*, Hodder & Stoughton, London, 2004.

12. Naglieri, J. et al, "Psychological Testing on the Internet: New Problems, Old Issues," APA Report, 2003.

13. Plimmer, G., "How to cheat a psychometric test", *Financial Times*, 3 April 2014.

Chapter 14:
Creating an optimistic firm

In this chapter we will cover:

- Why optimism is so important;
- The science of optimism; and
- The PACTS model of creating an optimistic firm.

At legal leader conferences in the US, UK, and Australia, as well as in the law firms we work with globally, we have been struck by the strong unease and even pessimism that seems to pervade at all levels. This is not surprising in the current climate of breathtaking change, small if any growth, and even constriction in the market.

Most legal leaders have read Richard Susskind's books, the frightening *The End of Lawyers* (2008) and the later, and even more frightening, *The Future of the Professions* (2015). We believe two things should be borne in mind: the future Susskind sees may not eventuate (predictions rarely do); and even if he is correct, there will still be the need for optimism if a professional services firm is to survive – no matter what business it finds itself in. We believe that many law firms are talking themselves and their profession into the grave.

Equally dangerous, many have their heads in the sand. Of course, firms will have to change, probably drastically, in the face of the rapid growth in robotics and artificial intelligence. However, as we show in the next chapter, there is the distinct possibility of a bright future in store.

What is certain is that, as John Denton, managing partner of Corrs Chambers Werstgarth commented, a law leader must increasingly become "a dealer in hope". In this chapter, we will show you how the latest findings in science can help you to create an optimistic firm that can innovate, adapt, and emerge stronger, be more resilient, and indeed hopeful.

Why optimism is important

It might be best to begin with a definition of optimism. Though there have been many definitions, the most widely used is "a mood or attitude associated with an expectation about the social or material future, one which the evaluator regards as socially desirable, to his or her advantage, or for his or her pleasure".[1] Note that this definition covers social as well as material expectations and the feeling that these are going to improve.

Pessimism is easy to sell. Newspapers and bloggers rely on it, and drug companies would likely go bust without it. Yet, to be successful and happy people need to be optimistic. On an individual level, optimistic people have fewer mood disorders, fewer health problems, they are (on average) richer, and they are more likely to be successful in their careers.[2]

Many studies have shown that optimists outsell pessimists. One study showed that optimists were 35 percent more successful in selling their product or service.[3] And yet, as a number of researchers have found, lawyers are more pessimistic than other professionals. As Seligman notes in his book *Authentic Happiness*, lawyers are 3.6 times more prone to depression than other professionals.

Pessimists are also less able to innovate or to adapt to new ways of working.[4] These are probably the reasons why law firms tend to lag behind many other professional service organizations in meeting the challenges of the new normal. In firms, the same dynamic applies. It is far easier to take a pessimistic line, particularly these days. It makes more of a conversation piece to say how terrible things are, especially when the less pessimistic view has, on the face of it, so little to support it. Yet, all the research shows that firms with a high degree of employee and lawyer optimism are more successful, and more able to adapt to the new circumstances than those that do not.[5] In fact, as many researchers have noted, there are optimistic and pessimistic organizations, just as there are optimistic and pessimistic individuals.[6] You can tell which category any firm falls into by listening to the talk in the hallways, or in the pub after work.

Pessimistic firms have a higher turnover of staff, lower engagement scores, and are much less likely to achieve their goals. In fact, there is a very strong correlation between optimism and engagement, goal achievement, and even strategic success.[7] Optimistic people tend to be more engaged and productive.

The job of a managing partner, and their executive, is to convey a sense of optimism in the firm. Not the obviously false optimism of the kind exhibited by CEO Andrew Grech after the shares in the listed law firm of Slater & Gordon fell from over $8 to under $0.60 in a short space of time in 2015. This will not encourage the engagement of either staff or shareholders. Rather what is needed is a *realistic* optimism. As best-selling author James Kouzes says in an *Ivey Business Journal* article: "[Leaders] are there to tell the team that they can succeed, that they can do it, that they have the will and the way to make it to the top. Not as a Pollyanna, but as a cheerleader. And, if necessary, credible leaders reassess the situation and find new ways to reach the goals or reset their original targets."[8] The ability to "reassess the situation and find new ways to reach the goals" is the cornerstone of business optimism. It is a realistic approach that is believable.

In our experience, many law leaders are optimistic; however, often their somewhat transactional leadership style and frequent, often frenetic, change initiatives, tend to increase the level of pessimism among their co-workers and staff, adding to the reluctance of partners to accept innovation. As Professor Bill Henderson of Indiana University has pointed out, without the backing of partners no law firm can change or innovate.[9]

TOP TIP

Ask yourself: Is my leadership style creating optimism or pessimism?

The science of optimism

Optimism is heritable – in other words, it has a strong genetic base (especially among women). In fact, all humans are naturally optimistic; we have what is called an "optimism bias". Nearly all children are born overly optimistic; it is part of what is called "magical thinking". If grandma dies, they believe she will be around again next week as usual. If a character loses a limb in a cartoon, it is only natural that it will grow another. We have noticed this in some lawyers who believe that the current changes in the delivery in law are just part of a cycle that will soon return to normal.

As a child gets older, magical thinking is usually replaced by a more realistic optimism. However, some children will naturally become more pessimistic – will tend to look on the darker side, to the glass being half-empty. Which way they go will depend to a large extent on whether they have the long or short version of the serotonin transporter gene. Those with the long version are the optimists and those with the short one are the pessimists.[10]

Which you have is a lottery. Alicia has the short version and Bob has the long one, which is why we often see the same events quite differently. And this is how nature intended it to be: a hunter-gatherer tribe needed both optimists and pessimists to achieve a risk/caution balance – as does a law firm. Creating an optimistic firm does not mean creating one in which everyone is an optimist!

Optimists tend to be risk takers, whereas pessimists tend to be more cautious. In evolutionary terms, this division makes perfect sense. Men tend to be more optimistic and adventurous and women more pessimistic and risk-averse.[11] On the hunt, which is inherently dangerous, optimism and risk-taking are in demand, whereas looking for what might go wrong is exactly right if you are gathering and minding children in an unpredictable environment.[12] Interestingly, because women are more risk-averse they also commit less fraud.[13]

The gene that predisposes us for optimism or pessimism is what is called a "soft" gene. This means that it can be influenced by the environment that a person is in. Optimism and pessimism are highly contagious. One of the first to notice this was the guru of positive psychology, Professor Martin Seligman, the author of *Learned Optimism*. Since then we have discovered that what is most easily learned is pessimism not optimism, but the idea of the contagious effects of the two remains valid.

This contagion is due to the action of the brain's mirror cell system, which allows us to feel what other people are experiencing. If we are surrounded by pessimists, we tend to become more pessimistic and the reverse is also true of optimism and optimists. This is one of the reasons that a firm, even one with optimistic leadership, can become pessimistic and thus unproductive and unable to adequately sell its services.

Creating an optimistic firm

Henderson, Susskind, and others have all hammered home the fact that law firms have to reinvent themselves and that, in the future, law firms will not look like traditional law firms. As Professor Henderson says, they may come to look more like vendors than professionals as does Lawyers on Demand, the legal equivalent of a temp agency. They may look like something else entirely. But without becoming optimistic they will die.

The good news is that recent research has shown us that any organization can become optimistic – even a law firm. The science shows that the process of creating an optimistic team, or firm, is relatively simple, but it requires planning and determination to successfully put into practice. The secret lies in what we call the PACTS model. The acronym stands for:

- Purpose;
- Autonomy;
- Collegiality or cooperation;
- Trust; and
- Strengths.

Purpose
Many studies throughout the world have shown that having a sense of purpose is at the very core of optimism.[14] However, it is a widely misunderstood concept. Leaders tend to think that lawyers and other staff should see the firm's purpose – to the extent that they have one except as a vehicle to make the partners money – as their own.

Humans are not built like that. To a human being, a real sense of life purpose – one that will reinforce optimism – must contain four essential elements:

- The purpose must, in all probability, outlast the individual's lifespan;
- It must have intermediate, achievable goals;
- It must be of benefit to society; and
- It must be pursued in the company of others.

There are some law firms whose purpose does satisfy some or all of these criteria. Many of the attorneys that work for Lieff Crabraser Heimann & Berstein (one of America's largest and most energetic plaintiff's law outfits), for example, certainly feel that their work there fulfills the four requirements. As one of their lead attorneys, Robert Nelson, puts it: "I've basically dedicated my life to trying to work to represent those who've been injured as a result, typically, of greed of the powerful."

In smaller law firms, the four criteria can be satisfied by the desire to ensure the survival and the continuity of the tribe, rather like members of the hunter-gatherer bands of old. However, once a firm has exceeded the number of people that a human can have stable social relationships with (as mentioned, this is 150 according to Professor Dunbar of Oxford University), then this no longer applies.[15]

But there are ingenious ways that a large law firm that does not have something similar to Leiff Crabraser's overall sense of being part of a fight for justice for the underdog can tap into a similar sense of purpose to increase their optimism. Law firms could use their pro bono outreach more creatively, rather as McDonalds uses Ronald McDonald House Charities. There is no doubt that the deep connection with the charity helps the hamburger chain with staff engagement, productivity, and an overall sense of optimism. The trick here is to get everyone involved in the charitable activity. Then the law firm work becomes the means by which its people are able to fulfill their sense of purpose.

CASE STUDY

During the recent Great Recession, we were working for the Australian and UK branches of a large multinational construction company. It soon became obvious that the company would not have enough work for all of its people, and their HR director was asked to arrange for the lay-off of about 25 percent of the workforce.

Bob was called into a meeting with the HR director and the then managing director. The MD was under pressure from the board to implement deep cost cutting in all areas. The HR director and Bob suggested an alternative to the lay-offs based on numerous recent studies showing that such lay-offs lead to greatly reduced productivity (up to 30 percent) from the remaining workers.[16] Since most of them would have to be re-hired when the economy picked up (as it quickly did for construction companies), and the cost of the redundancy payments would be very considerable, the lay-offs seemed an exercise in futility.

What Bob and the HR director suggested was that the staff would be offered a couple of alternatives. They could either take redundancy and go, or they could remain and work part time for the company and part time for a national charity of their choice. There would be a reduction in pay, but not a very significant one. The HR director and her team questioned those who chose the charity route and it became clear that they had a deep passion for the causes that they chose.

> The interesting finding that this experiment produced was that the charity group's work time productivity greatly increased. What's more, when the economic pick-up did come and these members of staff went back to working full time, the overwhelming majority continued to do charity work in their own time and their increased level of productivity remained. Those who ceased the charity involvement quickly returned to their previous productivity level.
>
> (Of course, the problem for most partnerships is that they rarely have enough of a cash buffer to invest in the way that large corporations have, so this particular option might not be available to them.)

Even activities that have nothing to do with the firm can increase employees' levels of optimism, which can spread to co-workers. Other studies have shown that those workers who are religious are more optimistic and have higher productivity levels. In fact, even the act of going regularly to a place of worship where you are in the company of others can lead to less depression and greater optimism. The sense of purpose and optimism of other members of the congregation is contagious.

TOP TIP

Ask yourself: How can I engender a sense of purpose in my firm?

Autonomy

A number of recent studies have shown that there is a strong relationship between personal autonomy and optimism. The same is true of a practice group, team, and a firm. The more control a person, a team, or a firm has over their own destiny, the more optimistic about the future they will be.

Autonomy will mean different things to different people, and leaders should never assume that they know what a particular person wants. To some it may be control over their working hours, to others a sense of being in charge of a project or matter. A few may want no control over their work life at all because the sense of control that they need resides elsewhere – perhaps in the home, in their sports team, or in their charity work. Autonomy really means being given the option and the power to choose without someone else's assumptions getting in the way.

Never assume you know what people need in terms of autonomy – always ask.

Commonality, collegiality, and cooperation

Humans are naturally cooperative. It's how we survived this long. We tend to cooperate best with those with whom we have the most in common. Firms that have a cooperative leader do best,[17] since that style of leadership is closest to our genetic preferences. It is one of those interesting things about us humans – the more in line our actions are with our genes, the more optimistic we become.[18]

And yet the most frequent question that we get asked by law firm leaders is: "How can I improve the level of cooperation among the partners?" How is it that so many firms have got themselves into the situation where they are asking for outside help in getting the owners of the firms to do what humans are naturally predisposed to do anyway?

We think that there are several, rather obvious, answers. The most obvious is that the remuneration systems that, historically, a large number of firms have been addicted to, are cooperation-killers. We are pack-hunting animals and yet partners have not been rewarded for doing so. The result has been that many partners cling onto clients as if they were a sinking ship's life ring and are reluctant to share work, even when it would be vastly to the benefit of both the firm and the client if they were to do so.

The second, which we alluded to earlier, is the leadership style of the managing partner, or the division or practice heads. If their style is transactional or dictatorial, then like children following the example of their parents, people will see this as the "right way" for the firm and non-cooperation will become part of the essential culture of the firm.

Thirdly, there is often little focus on what people who work for the firm have in common. Rather, there is an emphasis on the importance of difference and diversity. Diversity in a team is a good thing, but it only works if the team shares a lot of commonality as well. We do not cooperate well with people who we perceive do not share our goals, beliefs, or backgrounds, largely because we do not feel trust. We do not empathize with them, we do not feel particularly altruistic towards them, and we tend to resent their presence.

We can open ourselves to true diversity, and to cooperation, if we perceive that the others around us are, essentially, part of our tribe. The more that a law leader is able to encourage the discovery of commonality, the more collegiality and cooperation they will get among the partners and others. This does mean allowing for ample face-time and socializing because, in reality, that is the only way that humans share those small commonalities that seem so trivial and yet matter so much to the grey matter upstairs.

> **Get the systems and procedures that block collaboration in the firm out of the way and allow cooperation to flourish.**

Trust

Since humans are primarily social animals, and trust is an essential ingredient in all relationships, it is obvious that it is also an essential ingredient in creating optimism. We have covered trust in some detail in Chapter 9 so there is no real reason to go into detail here. It suffices to say here that a leader must use all of the five Cs of trust skillfully in order to create the foundation for optimism and make sure that they become part of the firm's behavioral framework. They are:

- Benevolent concern;
- Communication;
- Commonality;
- Consistency; and
- Competence.

> **Make creating trust at all levels of the firm a top priority.**

Emphasis on strengths

In Chapter 7 we talked about high-performance team dialogue – the way that high-performing teams converse with each other. One of the key elements of that is the use of positive statements rather than negative ones. When it comes to creating optimism in a firm, this focus on the positive is something that a leader has to concentrate on.

When people are acknowledged for their strengths rather than castigated for their weaknesses they become more optimistic – no matter what form of the serotonin transporter gene they were born with. In Chapter 10 we explained the power of praise, and how a culture of praise can raise a firm's productivity and profitability by over 25 percent. Praise is also vital for learning.

One of the reasons for this is that, as research has shown, people do not learn from their mistakes. We learn from repeating what we do right and getting rewarded for doing so. When we get that reward, neurons in the striatum and the ventral prefrontal cortex store the information and make it more likely that we will repeat the behavior. The best reward is praise or public acknowledgement.

The job of the leader is to catch people doing the right things, not look for what they are doing wrong. This is difficult for a lawyer because legal training predisposes one to look for what can go wrong – to look for the mistakes. Unfortunately, in behavioral terms this is precisely the wrong thing to do. This is not to say that you should never point out when people are making a mistake. What you should do is point out the mistake and then say what you need them to do differently in the future and praise them when they do it. It is also important to praise them for the attempt at doing the different action – not just when they succeed.

A Gallup Organization study showed that organizations that have a culture of praise are 20–25 percent more profitable and productive than those that do not.[19] Praise stimulates the brain to get dopamine and oxytocin flowing to the ventral striatum and the combination of the two neurochemicals is a potent stimulant for optimism.

TOP TIP

Make sure you catch people doing the right thing, not just the wrong one.

Conclusion

No firm will ever become totally optimistic – nor should it. An unreasonable optimism would lead it to irrational risk taking, just as it does in an individual. However, in order to survive in these times of the new normal, a fairly high degree of positivity about the future – or at least the tribe's ability to meet challenges well together – is essential. It is too easy to fall into gloom and with it the fear of change and innovation. Humans are naturally somewhat optimistic; most of us have what is called an "optimism bias", which a skilled leader can use to improve their firm's productivity and profitability.

In order to really take advantage of this inbuilt bias, a managing partner or any leader in a law firm has to adopt and practice the PACTS skills. It may not be easy – some of them go counter to lawyers' natural instincts and training – but the pay-off will be huge and may well be the difference between the firm's survival and its demise.

It would be a good idea if every firm leader had John Denton's phrase that a law leader must be a "dealer in hope" framed on their desk (assuming that they have a desk in the future). PACTS give people the feeling that their leader is such a dealer.

References

1. Peterson, C., *A Primer on Positive Psychology*, Oxford University Press, New York, 2006.
2. Peterson, C., "The Future of Optimism", *American Psychologist*, 55:1, 2000, pp 44–55.
3. Seligman, M., "Why are lawyers so unhappy?" in *Authentic Happiness*, Atria Books, New York, 2004.
4. Wunderley, L. et al, "Optimism and pessimism in business leaders", *Journal of Applied Social Psychology*, 28:9, 1998, pp. 751–760.
5. Medin, B. and Green, K., "Enhancing performance through goal setting, engagement, and optimism", *Industrial Management & Data Systems*, vol. 109: 7, 2009, pp.943–956.
6. Bruton, J., "Looking both ways: management structures and processes in organizations facing conflicting environments," *Journal of International Management Studies*, 12:1, 2011, pp. 36–56.
7. Jaesoo, K., "Managerial beliefs and incentive policies," *Journal of Economic Behavior and Organization*, Vol. 119, 2015, pp. 84–95.
8. Kouzes, J. et al, "A prescription for leading in cynical times", *Ivey Business Journal*, July/August 2004.
9. Henderson, W., "Three Generations of U.S. Lawyers: Generalists, Specialists, Project Managers", *Maryland Law Review*, 70:373, 2011, pp. 373–390.
10. Fox, E. et al, "Looking on the bright side: biased attention and the human serotonin transporter gene", *Proceedings of the Royal Society B*, vol. 1788, 25 February 2009.
11. Pluess, M., *The Genetics of Social Wellbeing*, Oxford University Press, 2015.

12. Bear in mind that not all hunters were men and not all gatherers were women.

13. Cumming, D. et al, "Gender Diversity and Securities Fraud", *Academy of Management Journal*, 58:5, 2015, pp. 1572–1599.

14. See e.g. Ho, M.Y et al, "The role of meaning in life and optimism in promoting well-being," *Personality and Individual Differences*, 48:5, 2010, pp. 658–663.

15. Dunbar, R., *How Many Friends Does One Person Need? Dunbar's Number and Other Evolutionary Quirks*, Harvard University Press, 2011.

16. See e.g. Sadri, G., "Reflections: The impact of downsizing on survivors – some findings and recommendations", *Journal of Managerial Psychology*, 11:4, 1996, pp. 56–59.

17. Gachter, S. et al, "Who makes a good leader? Cooperativeness, optimism, and leading-by-example", *Economic Inquiry*, 50:4, 2015, pp. 953–967.

18. Caprara, G. et al, "Human Optimal Functioning: The Genetics of Positive Orientation Towards Self, Life, and the Future", *Behavior Genetics*, 39:3, 2009, pp. 277–284.

19. Robinson, J., "In Praise of Praising Your Employees", *Gallup Business Journal*, 9 November 2006.

Chapter 15:
What are you really selling?

In this chapter we will address:

- The science of buying and selling;
- Professional services and the use of adult attachment theory;
- Finding a client's real needs; and
- Finally, we will summarize the new service to sell.

What are you really selling? Until recently, the answer to this question would have been obvious – legal services. It is not so clear now. Many of the services that a traditional legal practice dealt in – agreements, writs, contracts, and the like – are now available for download, or can be obtained much more cheaply and quickly from other sources. Others are being taken in-house or, increasingly, are being broken down into component parts that a computer can do.

An increasingly common belief nowadays is that artificial intelligence (AI), commoditization, decomposition, and digitization will probably make much of the work of lawyers – and indeed all professionals whether in-house or not as well as the firms they work for – redundant in a few years anyway. Law firms can either accept their demise gracefully or look around for some other market to be in, some other service to sell – rather like the large accountancy firms have done.

In this chapter we will explore what those other services might be. We believe that human science shows that there is another way besides lawyers becoming legal IT practitioners. Science is also offering a revolutionary approach to selling services. As always, in this chapter we will be deconstructing some cherished myths and proposing more effective alternatives.

The science of selling services

Lawyers hate to see themselves as salespeople, but at least at the senior associate or partner level, that is essentially what they will increasingly become. The 1980s and 1990s spawned a large number of sales methodologies. Some of these were based on the psychology of the day and others on little more than wishful thinking. We now know so much more about what prompts a human being to decide to buy goods or services than we did then. Essentially, we know now that however we buy – from a person or from the internet – the reason is always because of a human being, or more specifically because of a human relationship. And while some clients are trying to make the process more anonymous through focusing more on formal tenders, or even getting AI to do it, there is more often than not still a human influence around the process.

The science can be broken down into two elements: the science of *what* is bought and the science of *why* it is bought. Both of these have an impact on how law firms go about their business now, and how they will in the future. The "what" people will buy is based on the four fundamental drives that scientists now realize all humans have: for shelter, for sustenance, to reproduce, and for supportive relationships.[1] Everything that we seek to acquire is either one of these, or a subset of one of these. And there are literally millions of subsets, some obvious and others far more subtle. Some of the things we buy are enablers of one or other of these drives.

Legal practice is such an enabler. People do not buy law per se; rather they buy legal services to get another one of the drives satisfied. Regular clients will hire a particular lawyer, or firm, because they are invested in the relationship with that lawyer or that firm or in the relationship with someone else they want to impress who values that lawyer or firm.

"Our clients are buying a relationship with our people", says Michael Greene, managing partner of Henry Davis York, a long-standing and very successful Australian law firm. "Humans buy a relationship with other humans, with a person or a team. Our people have to form a partnership of mutual respect and understanding with their clients, underpinned by a very strong legal expertise."

In reality, it always was thus. The business of law was always based on forming relationships, only for many years there was a limited number of lawyers and an abundance of clients so the essential nature of the business was hidden from view. Lawyers thought that they were only selling their expertise and their knowledge when, in fact, those were assumed by the client. It is pointless to try to sell something that the potential client already takes as given. Overwhelmingly, the consumers of law were looking for exactly the same thing as people in a small town looked for in their family solicitor – a trusted advisor who knew them well and who had some knowledge of the law. Or, as Greene puts it: "Key advisors with a legal focus."

The mutually supportive and knowledgeable relationship between the lawyer and the client is what law firms sell. Increasingly, partners in firms are recognizing this and are turning their BD endeavors in this direction. In any mutually supportive relationship it is essential to really understand each other. This is not the old idea of the lawyer/client relationship, but something quite different. As Robert Regan, partner in charge, Sydney at Corrs Chambers Westgarth says: "The key issue is to genuinely understand the client's needs and how I can be a constructive participant in satisfying those needs. I try to be as generous as possible in understanding the client's agenda and drawing on my capabilities, insights, and networks to contribute to the client's success. If I am not able to do that, or the client does not value the contribution, it is hard to see how there can be the basis of a sustainable and mutually rewarding relationship."

The important word here is "mutually". Like all relationships, the relationship between a lawyer and their client is a complex mix of psychological and neurogenetic elements. In fact, the brain makes no distinction between a "professional", or "business", or "social", or even "family" relationship.[2] They are all, in a sense, a partnership in which people strive to satisfy a number of emotional, physical, and psychic needs. A client therefore, like any partner in a relationship, must add to the lawyer's sense of being supported in more ways than just providing fees for work done. Otherwise the mutual activation of the dopamine reward system will not happen and the relationship will not be established.[3]

Much is written about how sellers of professional services must meet clients' needs (the necessity of having a customer-focused organization), but the converse is also true. A client will quickly discern if the lawyer sees obtaining fees as the only value in the relationship and no other more basic needs are being met. If this is the case, danger signals from the amygdala (the fear center of the brain) will flash and they will back away. To the human system, a situation in which there is little mutuality is perceived as a danger and, to use Regan's word, is not "sustainable".

In reality, the fact that the lawyer has emotional and psychic needs of the client is one of the factors making the sale of their services possible.

The lawyer's rush to satisfy the client's needs without considering their own, or making them known to the client, is what kills many lawyer/ client relationships and makes it difficult to retain clients.

The "why" behind you buying a seat on one airline rather than another, or voting for one political party over another, or even buying branded or unbranded goods in the supermarket is largely determined by your genes and your childhood experiences. For example, if you ask customers why they buy Diet Coke or PepsiMax, as opposed to a super-market brand low calorie cola, they will probably tell you that they prefer the taste. Numerous experiments have shown that in blindfold tests few people can tell the difference. In fact, there is only one person we have ever met who could genuinely tell one cola from another on the basis of taste. He was a professional taster employed by PepsiCo who also raved enthusiastically about Pepsi's "bouquet of caramel". For the rest of us this decision, like so many others, is governed largely by our DNA.

It is the same thing with political parties. We are programmed by our genes to vote for conservative or radical parties.[4] Within that overall genetic bias we tend to vote for the party our parents, or someone else that we respect highly, voted for.[5] Pundits talk about "undecided" or "floating" voters who are supposed to decide elections. Along with many of our fellow scientists, we do not believe in the existence of these remarkable individuals. On the basis of many studies, we believe that their voting intentions have already been decided and all that remains is the rationalization of the decision.

Though there has been little neurogenetic research on what guides a client to choose the services of one law firm over another, there are some clues in the science which allow us to make a few shrewd guesses. For example, some firms have a strong brand, such as Coca Cola, and will probably attract people who are genetically geared to buy branded goods. Other firms might well play off the fact that they do not have a strong brand – they are the store brands and will attract those whose DNA drives them in that direction.

Another clue is the issue of people's risk tolerance. Human beings have differing appetites for risk. Our risk appetite is part of our DNA and it is very hard to overcome. We are naturally attracted to a firm that promotes itself as being in line with our genes in this respect. For example, those clients who are a bit more risk averse would probably choose a Magic Circle or BigLaw firm such as Linklaters. It is a long-es-tablished firm with a reputation for stability. These buyers are the same people who will buy a Volvo, fly Qantas, and perhaps shop in Harrods.

They believe that paying more for the purchase will reduce their risk. They are trying to buy certainty, and they will probably eschew online legal services, or a smaller less well-known firm.

Those with a higher risk tolerance might go for a smaller firm with more of a reputation for being "commercial". They might own a somewhat more adventurous vehicle, fly Malaysian Airways, and shop at an up-and-coming boutique. And they are more willing to purchase legal services online.

Of course, risk and relational reward are very closely tied together. What we fear most is the risk of damaging a supportive relationship. We might make a purchase decision we see as risky if, by doing so, we get a relational reward. A risk-averse man may buy a used MGB, thus going against his initial preference for the Volvo, in order to impress someone. Or a risk-tolerant client, who might personally prefer a smaller, more aggressive firm, may engage Freshfields in order to please or impress their board.

The greatest risk for a human being, no matter what their overall risk tolerance is, is always the loss of a real or potential supportive relationship, or nexus of relationships. This governs so many of our purchasing choices, including which law firm to engage.

> **TOP TIP**
>
> Ask yourself if you are a "branded" firm or a "store brand", and make use of that in your marketing. Decide which profile you want to target and go for that – it is unlikely that you can attract both.

Using adult attachment theory

"I do the worrying; I hold a client's hand throughout the litigation process. In a way I'm like a parent, offering protection, guidance, and understanding." This is the way that Grant Majorybanks, one of Australia's most successful litigators, describes his relationship with his clients.

In a very real way this quote sums up the basics of adult attachment theory, one of the most useful and most misunderstood ideas in marketing any service. The psychologist Edward Bowlby first came up with the idea of attachment theory in the early 1950s and applied it to the relationship between a primary caregiver and an infant.

The most important tenet of Bowlby's theory was that an infant needs to develop a relationship with at least one primary caregiver for the child's successful social and emotional development. Mothers, fathers, or any other individuals, are equally likely to become principal attach-ment figures if they provide most of the childcare and related social interaction. In the presence of a sensitive and responsive caregiver, the infant will use the caregiver as a "safe base" from which to explore.

According to David Howe, one of the foremost experts in this field of psychology, "even sensitive caregivers get it right only about 50 percent of the time. Their communications are either out of synch, or mismatched. There are times when parents feel tired or distracted. The telephone rings or there is breakfast to prepare. In other words, attuned interactions rupture quite frequently. But the hallmark of a sensitive caregiver is that the ruptures are managed and repaired."[6] If a child does not have "secure attachment" – if, for example, the caregiver is absent, or abusive, or neglectful – then the child will grow up fearful and unable to make good relationships later on.

For some time it was assumed that attachment theory only applied to infants. Then in the 1980s it was found to be equally relevant to romantic relationships and to explain why some worked and others did not, and it was finally applied to all significant relationships.[7] Recently, it has been shown that this attachment can explain an enduring relation-ship between any professional service provider and their client.[8]

In fact, the idea of secure or insecure attachment has been shown to be a major factor in any relationship where there is a power differential – as with a parent and a child. Yet, so many partners and lawyers get attachment wrong. They get the parent and child relationship the wrong way around. For example, most lawyers behave as if the client were the parent figure. After all, the client seems to have all the power – they can hire and fire their lawyers and, to a large extent, they dictate the fees. Faced with this, lawyers tend to adopt child-like supplication behaviors towards their clients and their potential clients. Firms twist themselves in knots trying to be "client-centric" in ways that would be amusing if they were not so expensive and pointless.

The reality of the relationship is quite different, as a number of studies with professional service firms have shown.[9] The majority of clients see their lawyer as the parental figure, the one who, in Marjorybanks' words, "does the worrying". They expect their legal advisor to act like a good parent – to have boundaries, to be interested in them as people, even to help them to succeed in their careers. In many cases a professional advisor will become a substitute parent upon whom the client will come to rely for advice, support, and counsel in many areas besides the law.

What does this mean in practical terms for a law leader or a partner? It means seeing clients in quite a different way. It means listening – as a good parent would listen – without interruption. Too often, in our experience, professionals are so caught up in their own expertise that they are constantly "reloading" (thinking of what they are going to say next), and so they do not hear the nuances of what their clients are saying, often missing clues to their state of mind, real needs, or fears and hopes.

Being the parent figure means asking more than telling in order to deeply understand the causes of their concerns, to help the client come to their own conclusions, and jointly to work out a course of action. In such a strong advisory relationship, the client may call on the lawyer's services as a sounding board, even if there are other sources of technical legal services available. There is no need to feel constrained from charging for acting as a sounding board.

In fact, giving away too much of value for free diminishes a lawyer's parental authority, and shows that they have few, if any, boundaries. One of the hallmarks of a bad parent is that they are too lax, and seem to have no boundaries. In the terrible twos and threes children often throw tantrums, seemingly to try to get their own way. They are really just trying to get their parents to lay down clear and consistent boundaries that they can rely on. Their safety depends on a parent remaining in control.[10]

A client is no different – though the tantrums may well take a different form (often quibbling about fees, or making unreasonable demands on the solicitor's time). A client-facing lawyer must be clear about what their needs are of the client and be prepared to articulate these in concrete and actionable terms. Eschew generalizations because these only lead to confusion and misunderstandings.

We were working with a large national firm in Australia on the issue of fees and partners were telling us that the management encouraged them to offer discounts of 25–30 percent almost as soon as a substantial potential client walked in the door. At the same time, they were rapidly losing market share and their profit per partner was declining.

One of our recommendations was that they cease offering discounts except in really exceptional circumstances. Naturally, they disliked the suggestion. There was a great fear that if they did not offer the discounts their rivals would grab more of the market. We replied that if they were

> only competing on price they were doomed, there is no profitable end to a price war – just ask the supermarkets. More importantly, for most people, competing on price gives a very negative perception as far as adult attachment is concerned.

Your fees are one aspect of your boundaries. But fees are not everything. There are other boundaries which, if crossed too often, delete a lawyer's parental authority. These may include demanding unreasonable deadlines, scope creep, and being emotionally used as a punching bag rather than as a sounding board. Or allowing your team members to be bullied or harassed. We know, for example, of one instance in a major firm where a female senior associate was discouraged from reporting a senior counsel of a major corporation who sexually molested her.

Not everyone is the same, of course, and attachment styles vary with childhood experience of parenting. Adults securely attached as children tend to have positive views of themselves, their partners, and their relationships, including with their professional advisors. They feel comfortable with dependence and independence – balancing the two. Anxious-preoccupied adults, by contrast, seek high levels of intimacy, approval, and responsiveness from their advisors, becoming overly dependent, but not always loyal or committed.

Dismissive-avoidant adults desire a high level of independence, often appearing to avoid attachment altogether. They view themselves as self-sufficient, invulnerable to attachment feelings, and not needing close relationships. These clients will be quick to dismiss advice, talk over their advisors, and generally make life difficult. They do this to suppress their fear of rejection, dealing with it by distancing themselves from lawyers of whom they often form a poor opinion. Fearful-avoidant adults have mixed feelings about close relationships, both desiring and feeling uncomfortable with emotional closeness. They tend to mistrust their advisors and view themselves as unworthy. Like dismissive-avoidant adults, fearful-avoidant adults tend to seek less intimacy and suppress their feelings.

A really skilled client-facing lawyer will be aware of and use these nuances to their advantage, building up a client base of people who feel at ease with the relationship. Despite all of these variations in attachment, the core fact is that the parent/child (advisor/client) relationship remains intact. The skills of asking, listening to the whole person, having positive regard, using praise, and having secure, concrete boundaries are vital in every client interaction.

TOP TIP

Listen to your clients to find out their attachment style.

Finding a client's real needs

Lawyers often assume that they know, sometimes intuitively, what a client needs of them. Very often they are wrong. In the same way they believe they know what value is to a client. Again, often they are mistaken.

Legal advisors often assume that value is what they have to offer, and that a client needs little more than their professional advice or opinion or purely legal work on the "matter". They could not be more wrong. You are not in the business of selling what you have, like an ironmonger in a hardware shop selling nuts and bolts.

Even the owner of a hardware store must make an effort to find out what their clientele needs and wants rather than assuming that it is whatever they happen to have in stock. Yet that is exactly what many lawyers and law firm partners do not do. Even those firms that have established client listening programs may fall into the trap of only listening to the client's needs regarding what they have in stock to sell – legal advice and action.

The value that you have to offer is not what you have in stock, but what the client wants and needs. Your value is not in the fact that you give them more partner time, that you are always available, or that you have a great deal of knowledge or experience. Or even, as one partner in a major international firm describes, that you always "tap dance for the client".

To find out what the client really wants you have to be willing to admit that all the knowledge, experience, partner time, availability, and "tap dancing" counts for very little if what you have is not what they are looking for, or what they need.

To find out what they need, and therefore to sell the right thing, you have to do two things:

- You must get to know their business almost better than they do; and

- You must ask questions to find out what their immediate and long-term goals are and what they need of you to meet them.

In tomorrow's marketplace, the competition will not only be the other law firms, but also the integrated professional service outfits such as PwC and the rest of the Big 4. Their selling point is that they will know the client's business because they are the businesses' accountants, strategists, productivity improvers, advisers on climate change and risk, and so on. They may even be good at "tap dancing". So it only makes sense, to them and to many of their clients, that they should be the enterprise's lawyers as well.

This may not work for everybody, but it will work for an increasing number of your clients. You cannot compete by sitting back and being "lawyers". You have to be able to add the commercial insights that the Big 4 do not, because you have thought about the situation differently, and at the same time you have to know the client's business just as well.

This will take time. It may mean that your firm, like Minter Ellison in Australia, goes head-to-head in some of the business areas (such as advisory) that the Big 4 has traditionally dominated. It certainly will mean your partners and lawyers getting out there and holding regular meetings with people at all levels of the client's organization. It will mean that you have to work out new ways of remunerating partners since it makes no sense to reward in the old ways when far more of their hours are spent in what used to be called "business development". You are not selling law; you are selling your ability to productively worry with the client. And to worry well, you must know the client and their business inside out.

A partner or other client-facing employee of your firm must be an expert questioner. They must be able to ascertain the real needs of the client, even when the client is not aware of them. The questioning must bring the client to realizations about their business that they otherwise would not have had. This is where value will lie, because any of these realizations may change the fundamental nature of the client's business.

In due course, almost all traditional legal services will have been commoditized, insourced, outsourced, digitized, systematized, and packaged. What cannot be "decomposed" is this ability to use questioning to find out what lies at the heart of the client's problems. This ability is uniquely human, and if you use it well, it is your greatest asset.

In the future, value will lie in this ability to use acute questioning to provide a positive impact on the client's business. It is here, and only here, that cost is not so much of an issue. This is certainly what your clients are telling us.

TOP TIP

When hiring legal staff, make sure that they have curiosity and are good questioners – in an interview, can they lead you to see your business differently?

Conclusion – The new service to sell

The new service is not law. Eventually, that will have been decomposed and stripped of almost any value. The partner of the future in a major firm will probably still have a law degree (although the managing partner may not), but they may not practice much law.

The service they will be selling will be a particular kind of relationship. It will be their ability to be a parental figure, a wise one who knows the client's business and industry so well as to be indispensable.

They will be the one who uses that knowledge not just to suggest solutions, but to ask the kind of questions that get the client to see their business in a new light and to arrive at their own new, and novel, solutions. They will be able to find out what the client's real needs are and to show clearly inconsistencies between those needs and the business as it currently is.

This is adding value.

References

1. Elstrup, O., "The fundamentals of Psychology, and the relation between psychologics and socio-logics", *ECCON 2006: Organizations as Chaordic Panarchies*, 2006.
2. The brain does see a romantic relationship somewhat differently, however.
3. Schultz, W., "Getting formal with dopamine reward", *Neuron*, 36:2, 2002, pp. 241–263.
4. Dawes, C. and Fowler, J., "Partisanship, Voting and the Dopamine D2 Receptor Gene", *The Journal of Politics*, 71:3, 2009, pp. 1157–1171.
5. Kelly, D., "Parents' Influence on Youths' Civic Behaviors: The Civic Context of the Caregiving Environment", *Families in Society*, 87:3, 2006, pp. 457–455.
6. Howe, D., *Attachment Across the Lifecourse*, Palgrave, London, 2011.
7. Rholes, W.S. and Simpson, J.A., *Attachment theory: Basic concepts and contemporary questions Guilford Press*, New York, 2004.
8. Farnfield, S., and Holmes, P., *The Routledge Handbook of Attachment – Theory*, Routledge, New York, 2015.
9. Rholes, W.S. and Simpson, J.A., *Adult Attachment: Theory, Research, and Clinical Implications*, Guilford Press, New York, 2005.
10. For more on this, see Murray, B. and Fortinberry, A., *Raising an Optimistic Child*, McGraw-Hill, New York, 2005.